MR. MOON

© 1999 Algrove Publishing Limited
ALL RIGHTS RESERVED.
No part of this book may be reproduced in any form, including photocopying without permission in writing from the publishers, except by a reviewer who may quote brief passages in a magazine or newspaper or on radio or television.

Algrove Publishing Limited
1090 Morrison Drive
Ottawa, Ontario
Canada K2H 1C2

Canadian Cataloguing in Publication Data

Stout, William B. (William Bushnell), 1880-1956
  The boy's book of mechanical models

(Classic reprint series)
Reprint of the ed. published: Boston : Little, Brown, 1917
ISBN 0-921335-88-1

  1. Toys–Design and construction. I. Title. II. Series: Classic reprint series (Ottawa, Ont.)

TT160.S68 1999   688.7'2   C99-900866-8

Printed in Canada
#10899

Publisher's Note

There are two problems with this book. The first is that it was published in 1917 and is far from being politically correct. It dwells fondly on stereotypes.

The second problem is that it assumes a near endless supply of wooden spools and cigar boxes, both of which are much harder to find today than they were at the beginning of the 20th century. Fortunately, many of the things once done with wooden spools can be done equally well with plastic spools or wooden dowel, both of which are in ready supply today. The cigar box presents a problem only in that a simple box must be made when a cigar box is not available. Other than these few points, the models in this book can be made as readily today as 80 years ago.

Whether or not the author's contention that one has only to "Give the real boy some tools and a workshop, and half the problem of bringing up the next generation is solved" is fully applicable today is a matter of judgement for the reader.

Leonard G. Lee, Publisher
Ottawa
September, 1999

THE BOY'S BOOK OF
MECHANICAL MODELS

SHOWING TOYS MADE BY BOYS FROM
DESCRIPTIONS INCLUDED IN THIS BOOK

THE BOY'S BOOK
OF
MECHANICAL MODELS

BY
WILLIAM B. STOUT

With numerous Illustrations

BOSTON
LITTLE, BROWN, AND COMPANY
1917

Copyright, 1916,
BY LITTLE, BROWN, AND COMPANY.

All rights reserved

Printers
S. J. PARKHILL & CO., BOSTON, U.S.A.

Contents

	PAGE
FOREWORD	vii
HOW TO MAKE A MECHANICAL DUCK	3
CIGAR-BOX AUTOMOBILE	7
A MODEL MOTORBUS	19
CIGAR-BOX RAILWAY LINE	24
CIGAR-BOX DUMP CAR	34
A CIGAR-BOX MONORAIL	41
AN AIR-LINE RAILWAY	47
A SIDE-HILL RAILWAY	53
TOY SCALES	59
A TOY CASH REGISTER	67
A TELEPHONE LINE	73
A TOY PHONOGRAPH	83
A WRITING TELEGRAPH	91
A TOY CRANE	98
A TOY TRIP HAMMER	104
AN X-RAY MACHINE	111
A SHADOW PICTURESCOPE	122
A MODEL GRAIN ELEVATOR	127
MODEL ELEVATORS	135
A PERPETUAL CALENDAR	157
A THRESHING MACHINE	165

CONTENTS

A Walking Horse	170
A Walking Policeman	177
The Pendulum of Galileo	184
A Siren Whistle	192
A German "Thur-Zither"	200
A Gutter Water Wheel and Dam	209
A Water Rocker	214
Some Interesting Mechanical Movements . .	219
Ocean Fun Ashore	225
Fighting Wild Irishmen	230
A Fighting Rooster Toy	234
A Climbing Bear	237
A Wiggle Bug	243
A Wooden Elephant	247
A Submarine Boat	254

Foreword

THE ideas included in this book have been collected during a number of years of work among boys. During these years the writer has discovered that a great many of the articles usually described for boys to make are very often impractical on account of the small size of the boy's pocketbook. All of those described in this book can be made from things picked up around the house, at no expense to the maker, while almost all of the toys are constructed with an ordinary cigar box as a base.

Everything described does some work or performs some peculiar function, a thing which has made the ideas of particular value to manual training schools.

The author wishes to thank the boys who have worked with him in the past for their share in the inspiration of this volume, and offers it to other boys of America in the hope

FOREWORD

that they may obtain from its pages an enjoyment equal to that he has had in its preparation.

It's easy to make things if you just will think and take pains. There is hardly any kind of a toy that you cannot make out of odds and ends you pick up around the house, if you will just use some ingenuity in putting the parts together.

Ideas are what the world pays for. Learn to get up ideas, and those of you young fellows, and smaller boys too, who start now to make things and to learn how to put parts together to get the result you want, are building the basis of business success.

There is too much old stuff in our ways of learning. The boy of to-day is more ingenious than his father, and is more handy at analyzing mechanical things. Give a boy a knife and some spools and a piece of tin, and he will make anything from a submarine to a flying machine, and the thing he makes will work when it is done. Many older men, by neglecting their mechanical instincts, have killed these possibilities in themselves.

Give the real boy some tools and a workshop,

FOREWORD

and half the problem of bringing up the next generation is solved.

The toys in this volume range from the submarine to a talking machine that talks, a grain elevator, a siren whistle, animals that move, musical instruments, etc. These toys can all be made with very few tools. The boys who read this and expect to make the things hereafter described should begin to save up odds and ends.

Every toy described will work if the directions are carefully followed, for the author has himself made all of them and has proved them to be successful.

If you want some fun the next time you go down to the lake, take some cigar-box wood and make a mechanical duck.

THE BOY'S BOOK
OF
MECHANICAL MODELS

THE BOY'S BOOK OF MECHANICAL MODELS

How to Make a Mechanical Duck

THIS is shown in perspective in *Figure 1*, and in section in *Figure 2*. You will better understand the principle from *Figure 2*. Here are shown the wooden pieces which make up the body part of the duck fastened to a wooden float *A*, with wing pieces on either side of the tailpiece. The neckpiece *H*, with the head, is pivoted between the wing pieces on a nail *p*, *Figure 1*, and has a lever *L* running out to the center of the duck to a point opposite a hole *O* in the center of the float *A*.

A wire runs through a nole in this lever *L* and down through the hole *O* into the water, terminating in a flat tin plate *P* either soldered onto the wire or held in place between two corks tightly slipped over the wire. A wire frame *w* arranged as shown acts as a guide for the wire *W*.

When you set this toy in the waves, the float *A* bobs up and down with the wave motion, while the plate *P* is resisted in its up-and-down motion by the water and alternately pulls or pushes as the float above rises or falls with the wave. A rubber band *r* at the top fastened between the lever *L*, and a nail *n* counteracts the weight of the plate *P*.

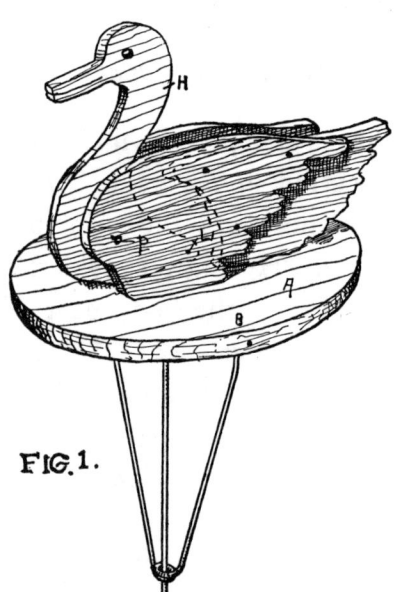

FIG. 1.

In making this toy, cut the float *A* out of inch wood, eight or ten inches in diameter.

On a piece of paper make a side view of the duck, with the invisible parts of each piece

HOW TO MAKE A MECHANICAL DUCK

shown dotted. This you may then trace, one piece at a time, onto the wood, from which you will cut the pieces.

Cut two of the wing pieces, marking out the pattern on cigar-box wood. Cut the tailpiece from half-inch wood. The head-and-lever piece is cut of cigar-box wood and pivoted in place on the nail *p*, which should fit loosely in holes in the wing pieces but drive tight through the headpiece *H*. A little paper washer or two should be slipped between the wing pieces and the headpiece *H* to keep them from rubbing together.

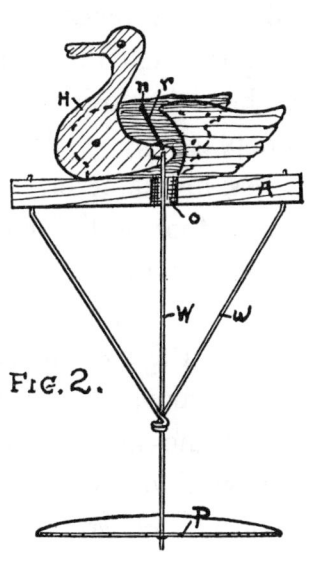

FIG. 2.

Bore a half-inch hole through the center of the float *A*.

Next nail the wing piece to the tailpiece, after which fasten this unit to the baseboard *A* just so the hole *O* is in the right position to receive the wire *W* when the headpiece is in place. Next, bend up the guide wire w with the loop at the bottom and stick the upper ends tightly through nail holes in either side of the float. Fasten the head in place after first looping the wire loosely through the hole at the end of the lever L. Slip the wire down in place through the loop in the guide wire, place the head in position, and then drive the nail p into place. Cut the disk below of tin about 6 inches in diameter, and let the wire W be at least a foot and a half long. As stated before, if you cannot solder, you may hold the plate P between two corks on the wire W.

Paint the toy all over so that it will not get water-soaked, being careful not to get paint in the moving joints.

Now if you will set the toy on the water on a windy day, you will have a lot of fun watching the duck bob its head about with each oncoming wave.

Cigar-box Automobile

IT'S surprising how quick people were to take up the automobile as soon as somebody really got down to work at it. It was a long time ago, though, years before the use of railroads, that people first thought of it.

Way back at the beginning of the steam engine, when machinery was just coming into use, several men worked at a scheme for attaching a steam engine to a coach — all traveling was by coach in those days, you know — and they made some pretty good machines too. A man named Hancock, and some other companies too, had a line of steam coaches running from London out to the suburbs. They were big affairs and weighed tons, but they worked and went eight and even ten miles an hour. They had regular boilers and burned coal or wood and made a quantity of smoke and dirt. In the Kensington museum in London I saw some of the drawings of these huge machines made at the time, and they are funny to us now, though they were fine for then.

Things were just getting into shape, and companies were starting to develop the machine to make it really worth something, when parliament cut off its own head and killed this industry by passing a law putting such a big toll tax on the steam coaches that the industry was completely put out of business, and Hancock's and Gurney's steam carriages were good only for scrap iron and chicken coops.

I saw too in that museum a little copy of Murdoch's model that he made to try out a scheme he had for driving a carriage on the road. He made only a small model about ten inches high and took it into the country just outside his village one night to try. It went so fast that he couldn't keep up, and the village parson, who happened to be in the way, was scared almost out of his senses.

The little machine, spitting fire and smoke and steam, came hissing out of the darkness straight at him, and he — as you can imagine — took to his heels. When he stopped, back in the village, he told, breathless, how he had been chased by the devil.

After this toll law put a stop to making engines to run on roads, all the time was spent on locomotives, and there wasn't much done toward real autos until just a few years ago. None of us grown-ups have to think back very far to remember the first automobile we ever saw. Why, it is only since about '89 that any one has made automobiles in the United States, and my! what a fuss they had trying to find a name for them.

The first machines were for passengers only, but you know how many things the automobiles are used for now. The only thing we have anywhere near like those old ones is the road locomotive, as it is called, — something like the threshing-machine engines you see dragging their loads around the country, only stronger.

From these down to the little fire-spitting motorcycle there are all grades and kinds of autos, — the great sight-seeing car, driven by gasoline or electricity, or both, and seating as many as fifty or a hundred people; enormous trucks carrying loads of many tons' weight; the large limousines and heavy touring cars which we see so often, — it seems as though there was no end to the attachments that may be added.

The racing cars are smaller in size than the automobiles that we see around town, but they are more powerful than any of the others. Then come the runabouts, and that nowadays may mean a high-powered machine as well as one of low power. In this class too come the delivery wagons, which are sometimes the same only with different bodies, and from this down there is only the little cycle car and the motorcycle, unless you count the toy machines sold in the shops and worked by the rider like a

CIGAR-BOX AUTOMOBILE

tricycle. The latest of these toys winds up with a spring and starts and stops with a foot pedal which is operated by the boy rider.

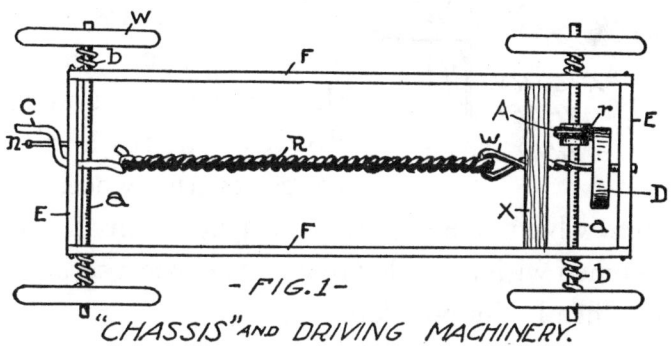

— FIG. 1 —
"CHASSIS" AND DRIVING MACHINERY.

In *Figure 1* is a toy model made of a cigar box. The frame is the size of the side of a cigar box and may be made of the same kind of wood, the pieces E and F being about a half or three quarters of an inch wide.

The shafts or axles a, running crosswise, may be of wood or wire passing through holes in the frame piece F with little twists of wire b between the wheels and frame to keep the wheels from rubbing.

The little back axle wheel A, if the axle is of wood, may be a piece of spool wedged on tightly. The wheel *D*, *Figure 2* — the friction wheel — is of half-inch wood, but round of course, and fastened to a wire axle twisted around as you see in the drawings, running double through the center of the wheel *D*, after which one end is turned up as at *L* and fastened with a staple *l* to hold the wheel securely and firmly in position.

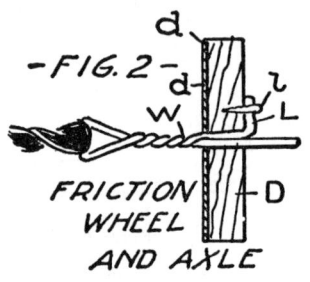

FRICTION WHEEL AND AXLE

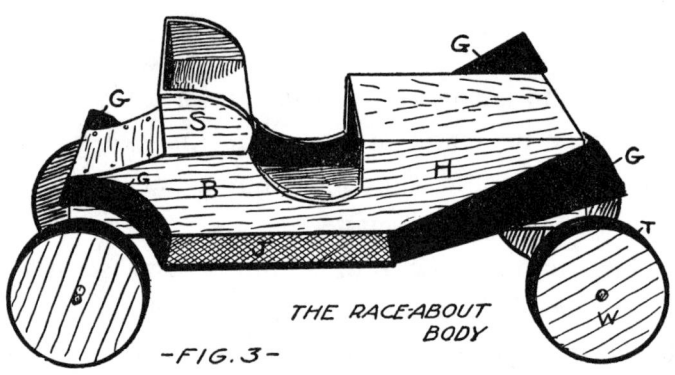

THE RACE-ABOUT BODY
—FIG. 3—

This construction may be clearly seen in *Figure 2*.

On the face of the wheel *D* is a piece of

CIGAR-BOX AUTOMOBILE

sand-paper, or rubber sheet *d*, to increase the friction between it and the small wheel *A* on the axle.

The wire shaft at the back of the wheel runs through a hole in the center of *E*, the back of the frame.

A crosspiece *X*, fastened in the position you see in *Figure 1* and through which the twisted part of axle *w* passes, forms a second bearing in a hole or vertical slot.

At the front of the frame is the wire crank *C* with its hook, between which and the wire shaft *w* at the rear the rubber bands *R* are fastened, and you can see too how the brad *n* is fixed to keep the crank from turning backward.

If you want to make rubber-tired wheels and can use a soldering iron to solder on wire axles, you can make your wheels of tin, like *Figure 6*, cutting little slots all around the edge and then bending the flaps so formed first one way and then

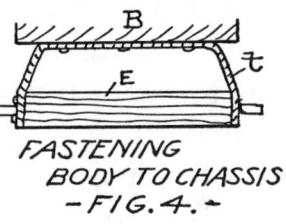

FASTENING BODY TO CHASSIS
-FIG. 4.-

the other, as at *h*, after which you can slip on a rubber teething ring *g* for the tire, or a bunch of rubber binders, the wheel having been, of course, cut out to the proper size.

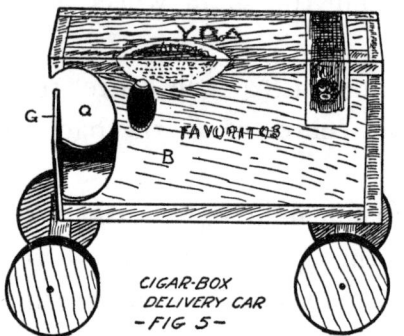

CIGAR-BOX DELIVERY CAR
-FIG 5-

The wire axle will be soldered through the hole in the center.

In *Figure 3* is a runabout body cut from a cigar box set on edge, — with keyhole or fret saw. It won't take the whole height of the box, and after you have sawed out the shape the seat and the top of the hood are made out of the pieces left. The seat should be a little longer than the box part *B* is wide.

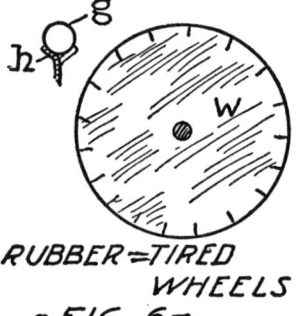

RUBBER-TIRED WHEELS
-FIG. 6-

Figure 4 shows you how to fasten the body to the "chassis" by a strip of tin *t*, and this needs no explanation, for you easily can see how it is done.

In *Figure 5* is shown the delivery wagon.

CIGAR-BOX AUTOMOBILE

The cigar box is made into a delivery wagon by cutting out the oval windows and the curves at the front of the box, leaving on the part *G* for a dashboard.

The wheels are of quarter-inch wood with flat rubber bands stretched around the rims for tires.

Figure 7 shows another type of delivery body which is easy to copy from the drawing. The wheels are of cardboard with cork hubs.

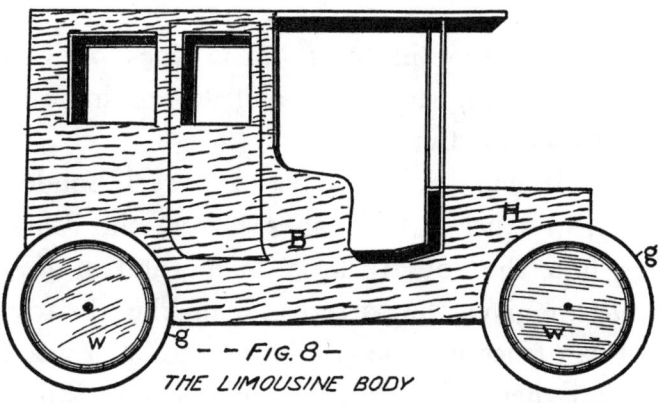

Figure 8 shows the hardest kind of body, a limousine, and this one is set right down onto

the chassis without any tin between. It is the hardest one to cut out with the windows and all, but when done makes the prettiest model. The only extra attachments are the pieces sup-

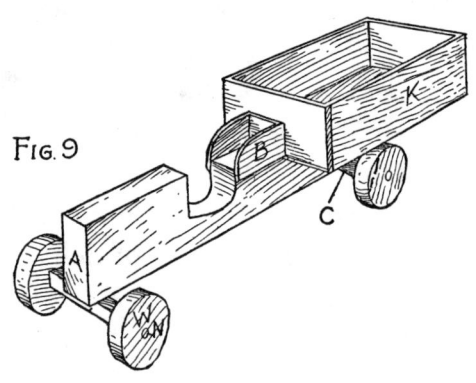

porting the roof in front. The lines on this body are merely for looks and do not indicate a real door or divisions.

The drawing *Figure 9* is of a real London Lorry, or truck. You can see from the drawings how the toy truck is made, and in *Figure 10* are given the patterns for making the toy. You can trace off the patterns onto inch wood and cut them out with a keyhole saw or knife.

The body *A* is of inch wood cut as shown, and has a hinge behind at *H*.

CIGAR-BOX AUTOMOBILE

To the back part a cigar box K is fastened to the hinge H so it can tip, only the greater part of the box must be forward of the hinge.

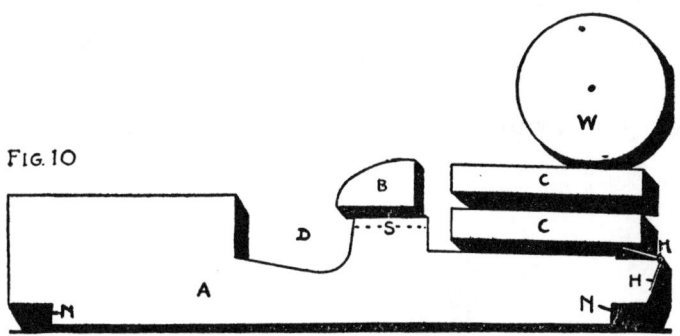

FIG. 10

The axles C are of wood, squared off to fit the notches N at the ends of A.

They are fastened crosswise as shown, and the wheels, which are also of inch wood, — or

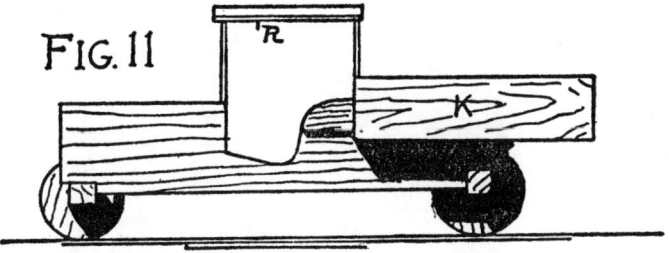

FIG. 11

can be carpet-sweeper wheels, — are pivoted at the ends by a nail or screw.

The seat sides are fastened at *S* and are patterned at *B*. The size of the hind wheels is given at *W*. The front wheels can be a trifle smaller.

The small sketch *Figure 11* shows a side view of the completed auto lorry and shows also how a roof awning can be added if desired.

A Model Motorbus

THE London Motorbus, originally a real institution, has degenerated into a military unit. It is none the less fun, however, to construct a model motorbus out of a cigar box, using cracker-box wood for part of the work and for the wheels.

Figure 1 shows the side view of one of these busses with the space for the driver up front and curved steps leading up to the roof at the rear.

In the first place a baseboard E is cut of cracker-box wood about half again as long as a cigar box and the same width as the box set on edge. The box itself is cleaned of paper and the windows on either side marked in and cut out. The box is then nailed onto the baseboard E.

Next, a roof board C is cut a trifle wider than the cigar box and several inches longer, so that when it is nailed on top, as shown, the front end will project out as a roof over the driver. This is also nailed in place, and a block *D* is nailed into the corner between the base *E* and the box to form the driver's seat. The hood *H* up front is made of a curved piece of tin and has under it two curved pieces of

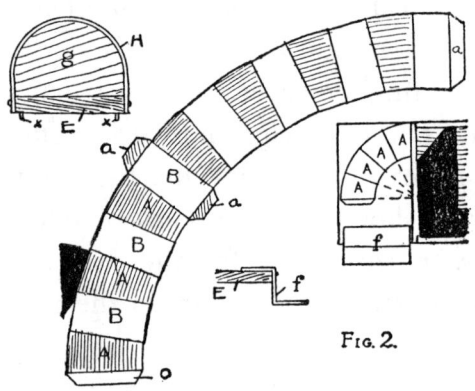

Fig. 2.

wood shown at *G* in the small sketch in the top of *Figure 2*. These end pieces *g* are nailed to the baseboard *E* and the tin is curved around them as at *H* to form the hood. On the side of the one next the driver's seat is nailed a rectangular dash piece, from which a steering pillar arises with a small wooden or cardboard wheel *e* at its top. At the rear are curved steps made from an enlargement of the

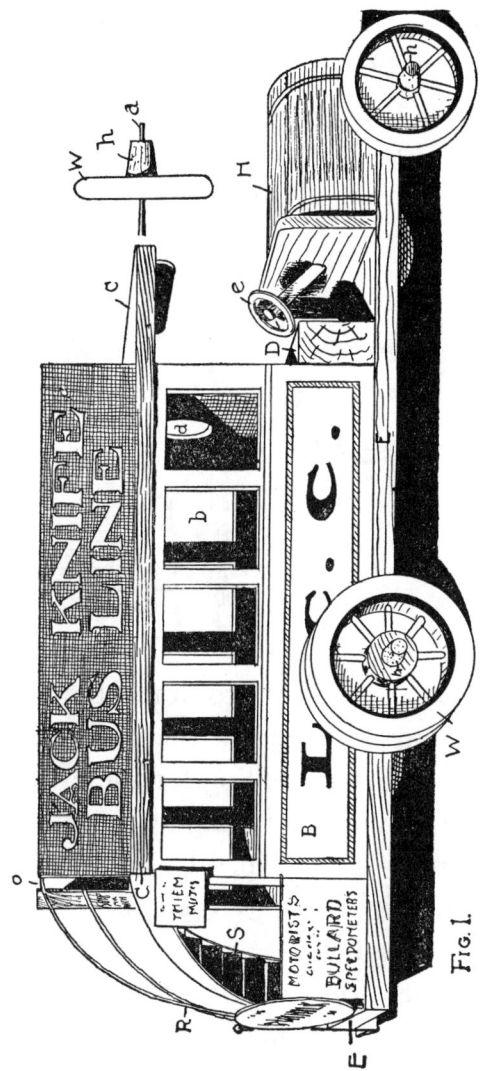

Fig. 1.

COMPLETED CIGAR-BOX MOTORBUS

pattern shown in *Figure 2*, and when you fold this up it will form the steps in just the curve you want, the parts *A* lying flat and the alternate parts *B* standing vertical to form the rise of the stair. A small piece of tin *f* is bent

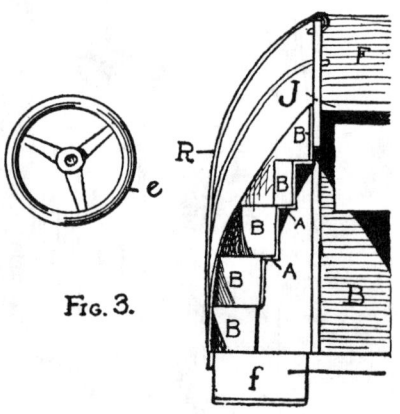

Fig. 3.

as shown in *Figure 2* to form the lower step. Wires *R* are arranged in the position shown in *Figure 3* to form a railing for these stairs, while now you may run a railing of tin all around the upper story as shown. If you like, you can add some tin seats to the roof, although this is not necessary.

The axles for the car are made of wire — heavy hairpin wire might do — running through bearings made of staples X driven into the under side of the board E as shown in *Figure 2*. The wheels are made of wood, or may be old carpet-sweeper wheels, but if you use these you will want larger axles than hairpin wire. They could be made of tin, or even heavy cardboard, if you did not expect the car to carry much of a load. Pieces of cork on the outside of the wheels make a very realistic hub.

With this much start, you should be able to develop as a toy quite a motorbus, and if you do not want to confine yourself to cigar boxes, you can make a larger model, using the wheels off your express wagon.

Cigar-box Railway Line

I HAVE already told you how to make a toy automobile, but this is going a step farther, being a description of a complete railway line, with its engine, truck, freight cars, and coaches, all made from cigar boxes.

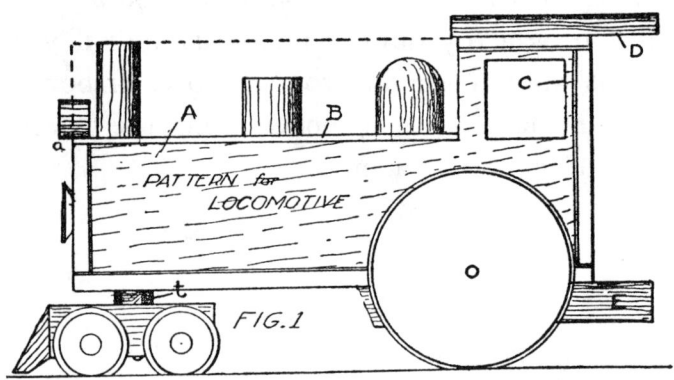

FIG. 1

We will make the engine or locomotive first, and I've drawn one in *Figure 1*.

Pick out a pretty long cigar box, — they are not all the same size, you know, — and with a saw, being careful about striking nails, cut down the length of the box on a line drawn two inches in from the edge, and cut this to within two and a half inches of the other end, where you saw a line down to meet it at right angles, so that when this is done you can take the piece out and the box will be left the shape of the piece *A* as in *Figure 1*.

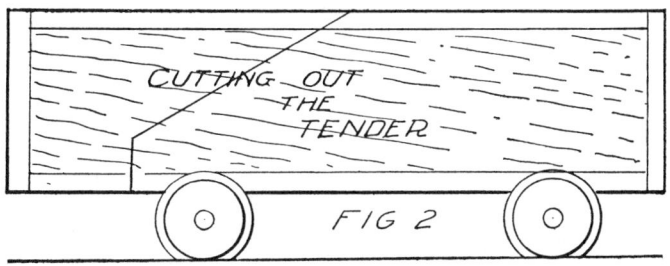

The part sticking up at the back at *C* is the cab, and you can cut out the windows with a sharp knife or fret saw, or just mark them out as you wish.

The top of the boiler is covered by a strip of cigar-box wood *B* where the opening was left in cutting out the dotted portion of the box.

The roof of the cab is made more realistic by fastening on a piece *D* of half-inch wood cut a little wider than the top of the cab, so that it can stick over the edges a little to form "eaves," and an inch and a half longer than the cab top so that it can stick out backwards over the platform *E*.

This platform *E* is a piece of inch wood as wide as the bottom of the box and fastened on underneath to look like the firebox and to stick

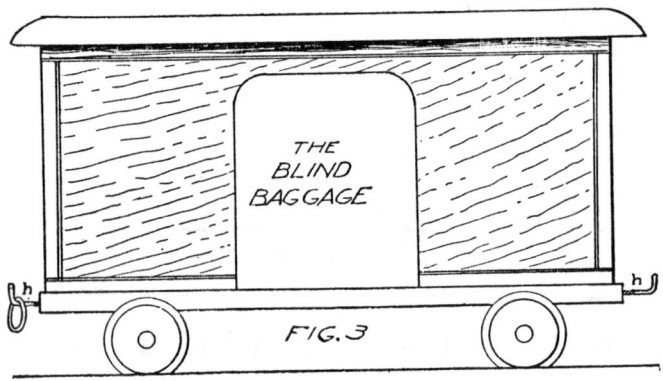

FIG. 3

out in back for a platform. The cab roof and this platform should stick out about the same distance.

The next thing to do is to make the front truck as in *Figure 8*.

Here you can see how the inch block *T* is shaped with the "cow-catcher" at the front and the hole *O* at the center between the wheels through which a screw runs up through some washers of cigar-box wood as shown at *t*

CIGAR-BOX RAILWAY LINE

in *Figure 1* and into the bottom of the boiler up front.

The wheels are halves of common spools turned around so the flanges are in and are fastened on with small screws that fit the center hole of the spool, or they may turn on little wooden axles of a width to suit the gauge of your truck.

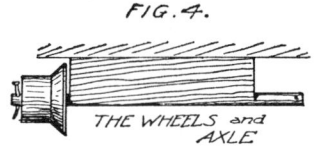
FIG. 4.
THE WHEELS and AXLE

The big back wheels you can cut out of half-inch wood, with a piece of tin cut in a little larger circle and tacked on the inside to form the flange; this kind of a wheel will do very well if you are good at cutting circles.

Another way is to take two blacking-box covers, or the boxes themselves, so long as both are the same size, and, holding the rim on the edge of some surface, such as the edge of a vise, as in *Figure 5*, strike the edge lightly over the edge of the vise, turning the can around as you work, until the

FIG. 5
MAKING the BIG WHEEL FROM A BLACKING BOX.

whole edge is turned over into a flange. Then inside this cover fasten a cross stick *a* with brads and through this bore the hole for the axle.

The two wheels can be connected by a round wooden axle through holes in the box sides, or they can be mounted on a wire axle. If they are not too big, you might mount them on round-headed screws screwed into *E*. Be sure the hole for the axle, wherever it is, is just high enough up, and that the big wheels will be in a line with those on the truck up front, so they will all track.

If you want to add cylinders and machinery to the engine to make it more like a real one, you can mount spools at the side of the boiler up front, as in the drawing of the whole train, and run wire connecting rods from them to a small brad crank on the drive wheel as shown.

The locomotive tender is cut from a common cigar box, like *Figure 2*, the line through the middle showing how it is cut. The wheels — spools, as in the other case — are mounted on the wooden axle as in *Figure 4*, and fastened with a pin at the outer end so they won't slip off.

CIGAR-BOX RAILWAY LINE

The blind baggage car, next in line, is made from one of the big square boxes. The roof is cut of half-inch wood curved at the ends, as in *Figure 3*, and rounded off at the sides too, only not quite so steep.

This piece should be cut big enough so it will stick out an eighth of an inch on either side and a quarter of an inch on the end; that is, it must be a quarter of an inch wider and half an inch longer than the top of the box. It is fastened in place with small nails.

Before putting it in place, however, cut the doors of the car, being careful to get them in the center and the same size.

On this car, in *Figure 3*, is shown one way of many that you can use for coupling the cars together. Hooks are screwed into the car ends at *h* and then a ring of wire is used to connect the two hooks. There are many other ways that you can do this, and I am only suggesting this one. Perhaps you can think of an automatic coupler.

The flat car is easy to make and is only a common small cigar box with the wheels fastened on their axles near each end — that is,

BOY'S BOOK OF MECHANICAL MODELS

a quarter of the length of the box in from each end.

Next comes the freight car, and this is a little more of a job. I have shown it in a separate drawing in *Figure 6*.

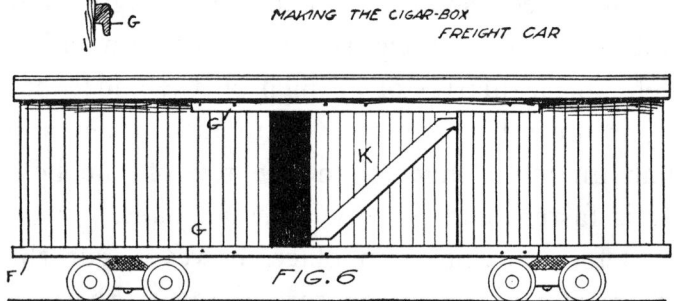

For this you take two large cigar boxes of the same size. This is going to be a good-sized car, so you had better get some wood from a cracker box to help out.

Knock an end out of each box and connect them with a board *F* running the entire length of the bottom of both and holding them about three inches apart to form the side doors.

On either side, at the top and bottom, nail sticks *G* shaped in section like the little upper sketch of *Figure 6*, so that when you cut out two little wooden doors of the cigar-box wood,

CIGAR-BOX RAILWAY LINE

as at *K*, they will fit in and slide between these strips, while at the same time the strips act as connectors for the boxes.

You can nail on the slanting piece to brace the door if you want to do so.

The roof of the car is made of a piece of half-inch wood, sticking out a bit all around and slanted off with a plane so that it is highest down the middle line of the roof, and will thus shed the rain.

At each end of the car cut a small window, shown in the car in the train drawing, and then fasten on the roof piece with brads.

The brake wheels can be made of checker men, and the brake shafts of wire. The brakes can be put on or not as you wish, though it is doubtful if you will use them if they are on.

This car is too long to work with the wheels arranged as the others have been, so we will make two trucks like *Figure 7* or *Figure 8* with four wheels to a truck and we will pivot each truck to its place on the bottom of the car by a nail or screw up through the hole *C* into the car bottom. Each truck will be fastened a quarter of the length of the car in from the end.

Be sure you get *B*, *Figure 7*, in this truck of the right width, — the same as *T*, *Figure 8*, on the engine, — so that the cars will run on the same track as the engine, and all cars stay on the track on the curves.

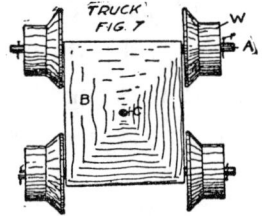
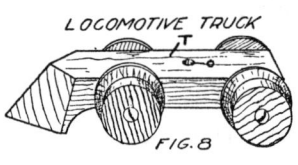

The passenger car is made a great deal like the freighter: of two big boxes end to end, only with no space between, for there are no side doors.

The rest of the passenger car I leave you to work out, for it is much the same except that windows are cut on the sides and doors on the ends.

You can arrange a track of laths and draw your train with a cable or cord between the tracks, or run it by a water motor or steam engine if you have one. There are many things also that you can add, according to what you have to work with and your own ingenuity in devising them.

CIGAR–BOX RAILWAY LINE

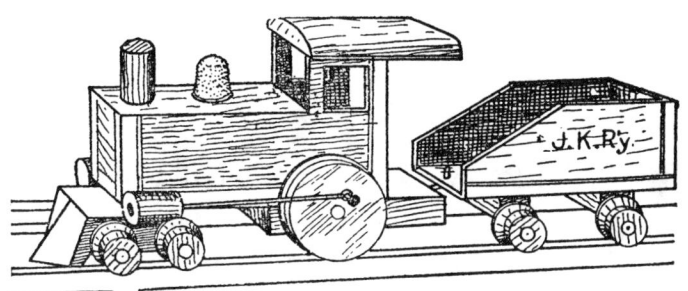

Complete Train of Cigar-box Railway

Cigar-box Dump Car

EVER own a railroad? I did once. It ran the whole length of our cellar and would carry freight in great shape. It wasn't a passenger line, and there was no real locomotive, but it provided lots of fun nevertheless.

The cars were copied from some I had seen used in filling in a cut along the railroad track near home, — dump cars pulled by mules, — and they dumped the load just as well as the big ones they were modeled after, only the load wasn't so big, of course, and they weren't pulled by a mule.

How were they made? I'll tell you in just a minute; only remember that it isn't necessary, when you make any of these things, to make them exactly as described. I give you the scheme and the principle to work on, show you how the scheme works, and tell you what kind of wheels I used, but if you happen to have some big spools, from some mattress fac-

CIGAR-BOX DUMP CAR

tory, for instance, you couldn't use a cigar box for the body. You'd want a cracker box or something larger.

Invent your own way of making the toys to fit the materials you have. If you can't get spools for the wheels, cut sections from an old curtain pole and put on circles of tin to make the flanges, so that the car won't run off the track; but, anyway, invent an article to fit your materials and the tools you have to work with.

I'll tell you the simplest way I know, and the most common things to make the toy of; then you can go ahead and do better if your tools and materials will permit.

To make a dump car like *Figure 1*, — and you can make a string of them if you desire, — get an empty cigar box, a couple of large spools, some tin, and some thin wood from the side of a cracker box, or the like, — wood about a quarter of an inch thick.

After soaking the paper off the box, knock it apart and remove the sides *D*.

Nail the ends *B* on securely, and then fasten the sides *D* in place again, only pivoting them on one small brad *n* at each end, so they'll turn between them to open out, as shown in the drawing of the car complete. The side on the further part of the car is shown swung open.

With an old pair of scissors or some tin shears cut a couple of strips several inches long and a quarter of an inch wide from an old oyster or tomato can.

Bend these up like *C* in *Figure 5* to form a catch and tack them to the end of the box with small brads so that the catch part *c* will

CIGAR-BOX DUMP CAR

hold the door or side *D* shut. These are shown at *C* in *Figure 1*. The brads that fasten them to the box should be back toward the inner end of the tin, so as to allow plenty of "spring," for we have to pull these back when the car dumps, so that the door *D* can open.

But now let's get at the truck.

First cut your two spools, which should be the same size, in half, taking care to cut them straight.

This will supply you with four wheels with flanges, and all you need to do is to turn the flange in to make them into good car wheels.

Each pair is mounted on a wooden axle cut like *F* in the drawings. The middle part, you see, is like a "V" turned upside down, only wider and with the high part in the center.

At the two bottom corners round axle parts *r* stick out, cut to fit the holes in the spools loosely and to stick clear through the spool halves. These axles should not be longer in all than the cigar box is wide.

Outside of the spools, pins *p*, *Figure 4*, are stuck through the axle to keep the wheels from coming off.

When you have two of these ready, connect them with a stick f several inches shorter than the cigar box, as shown in *Figures 1, 2,* and *3*.

Next make two other triangular-shaped pieces like F, only with no axles on the corners. These are shown at A in the drawings. They should be made of the same sized wood as the pieces F and about the same shape, and just the length of the box, as shown in *Figure 3*.

Fasten the pieces A to the bottom of the cigar box with brads and far enough apart so that the pieces F of the truck frame, that the wheels are fastened to, fit just between, as in the drawing.

Now you can bore a hole through the piece A near the bottom of the V, and drive a brad or shingle nail through it into the piece F at the top of its V. Or you can make a hole through both and run a wire through the entire length of the car, as in *Figure 2*. If you drive the brad or nail in, hold a weight behind F while you do it to keep it steady.

Your car now begins to look like something, only the box tips all ways and won't stay up. We can easily fix that, however.

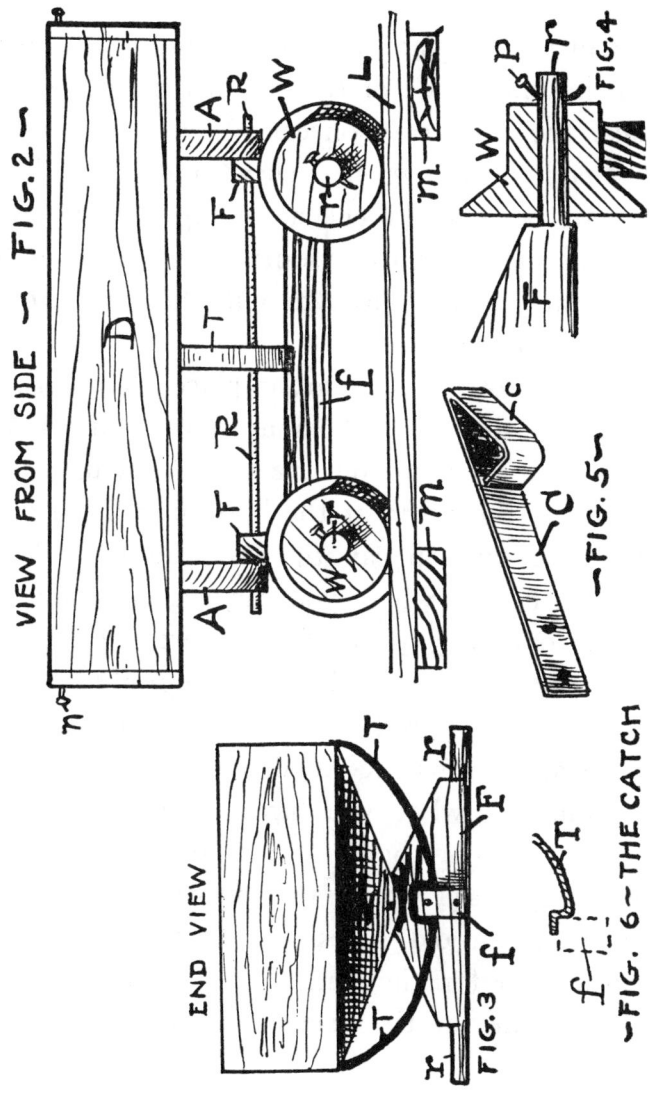

Cut two strips of stout tin T and fasten them to the under side of the car in the middle and near the outer edge on each side.

Bend them down in a curve and with a little square bend in the end as in *Figure 6*, to catch on the piece f in the middle of the truck under the car. You'll have to cut them to proper length, of course.

When both of these are in place, as in *Figures 1* and *3*, the car is held upright for its load.

If you push up on one tin T, though ever so little, the catch at the bottom is lifted off f and the car top can tip and dump the load.

And here is where you can get busy and invent something yourself, for there are a dozen different ways to hold the box upright.

The track can be of laths or tin strips on edge and with little wooden ties m across, depending on what you have to make it with.

If you know how to cast in lead, you can make yourself some fine wheels by casting them in an old blacking box with the edge turned up for the flange and a wire through the middle for the axle.

A Cigar-box Monorail

SOME years ago a man in England invented a new kind of railway, one which runs on only one track, which is called the Gyroscope Railway.

What is a gyroscope? As near as I can explain it to you, it is a top constructed so that it can turn in any direction; that is what the ones you buy on the streets are. Generally the word is used as a scientific term to represent a rotating wheel fixed to illustrate the laws of rotary motion. You see, if a wheel is turning fast, it is hard to move it out of its path, for it wants to stay always in the same place. If you hold a bicycle wheel by its axle and start it whirling, you can let go on one side, and the wheel will hold itself up while it is turning.

This is the scneme the Englishman uses to keep his car from upsetting. He has two wheels revolving in opposite directions, and as these will stay in the same plane all the time, — so long as they turn fast enough, — by a proper mechanism, they keep the car upright as long as they spin.

Now it is no easy task to make a gyroscope, and the ones in the toy shops are not heavy

enough to balance more than their own weight; thus to make a railway, you would need to have two gyroscopes and would require some arrangement whereby each would rotate just as fast as the other. However, I can tell you how to make a car that will run on a single suspended track, and it will look like the gyroscope car.

The drawing *Figure 1* shows the car run-

A CIGAR-BOX MONORAIL

ning on a stretched wire as a track. The drawing *Figure 2* is a front view, showing a track fastened to the wall and the way the counterweight hangs.

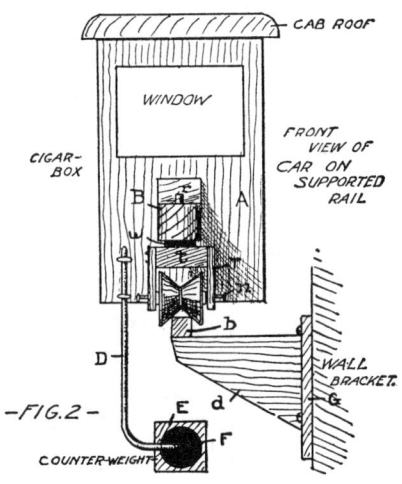

The car body is made of a cigar box, and *Figure 4* shows how the box is cut. The piece *f* is cut out entirely and thrown away, and the squares *e* are cut out to make the windows. There's a window in the front too the same height as these and nearly as wide as the box. This picture shows the side of the box set on edge. You can use a big square box if you like.

This done, cut out a roof piece *R* big enough to stick out around the edge a quarter of an inch or so and rounded off on top. The separate drawing *Figure 3* shows how to make the trucks. These are very simple and consist only of a piece of wood *t* a little over half an inch wide and a couple of inches long, cut from a

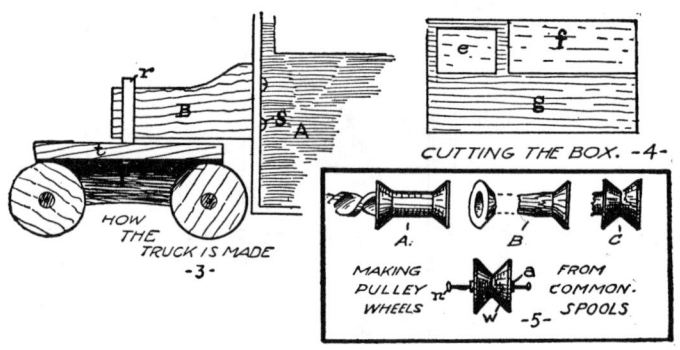

piece of half-inch wood. Pieces *T* of thin wood or tin run down from the sides of this piece and between these the wheels are mounted to turn.

Figure 5 shows how the wheels are made:

Take four common spools, all the same size, and treat each one of them as in the drawing. First, with a bit just the size of the middle part of the spool bore a hole in one end, being careful to center the bit right; when the bit comes

A CIGAR-BOX MONORAIL

through, you will have one edge of the spool in a ring around the bit, as at *B*. Here too you see the shank of the spool that's left whittled down so that it will slip through the hole in this "doughnut" you have cut off. The third stage will be that of *C*, and all you have to do is to cut off the edge sticking beyond. Then put a wooden axle tightly through the hole in the spool center and drive a brad in the center of each end. These wooden axles *a* should be just long enough to fit between the pieces *T* as in *Figure 2*.

At each end of the car body a piece of inch wood is now fastened, shaped as shown at *B* in *Figure 3*, and fastened with screws *S*.

A nail or screw through a hole in *B* goes down into the center of the top piece *t* of the truck, and the truck is mounted. Be sure it turns free and that the wheels don't hit the box.

The counterweight that hangs below *C*, *Figure 1*, is made by boring a hole three-quarters of an inch in diameter through a block of wood as long as the car body. Then string the wire *D*, *Figure 2* through and, resting one end of the block in sand, fill the hole with lead, burying the middle part of the wire in it.

When cool, the wood may be split off entirely or planed down square, as in the drawing, *Figure 2*.

The wires sticking out of the ends are bent and fastened to the car, as shown, so that the weight will hang directly below the center of the car. By putting the support at one side quite a distance and then bending the wires in down below, you can make a track hang on brackets, as shown, so that your car lines can run around the sides of your shop with turns at the corners made of tin. The track *b*, *Figure 2*, may be made of laths.

An Air-line Railway

IF there is a boy just across the court from your flat, or in the next house, to whom you want to send messages or any light merchandise, here is a railway that runs on a string or cord that will furnish all the fun you would want, and at the same time be a practical way to send things back and forth, provided you fix the "air line" across the court or some space where it will not interfere with traffic.

The railway will cost you only your time, as all the things needed to make it are common about the house.

The main part is a cigar box for the body part, then some bits of stout wire, some pine sticks, a piece of curtain pole for the pulleys, some stout cord, and some scraps of board.

From the frame, which is formed of two side sticks F and a central space block, as shown at b, wire supports W hang down. These pass through holes in the frame, as shown at the top, and then, dropping on either side of it, end in hooks which stick into holes in the sides of the cigar box.

Thus the box is supported from the frame, and the weight of the whole structure is brought low, so that the pulleys cannot upset on the cord line or track.

The cord, which runs under the pulleys, passes around a pulley D supported to turn at each end of the line. The drawing shows this pulley mounted on a wall outside, where it can easily be reached. This pulley has a crank on the side.

Passing over the top of the pulley at either end, the cord line runs back underneath and finally ties to the box through holes bored for the purpose. In tying here the line is drawn tight.

The end pulleys should be made large if you want to get any speed out of the car, but if you expect to carry weights of any size use a smaller one.

When both pulleys are arranged to turn easily and are made readily accessible to the opera-

AN AIR-LINE RAILWAY

tors at either end of the line, we are ready to see how the scheme will work.

You can easily see that when you turn the crank at one end of the line the cord will pass over and back, or vice versa.

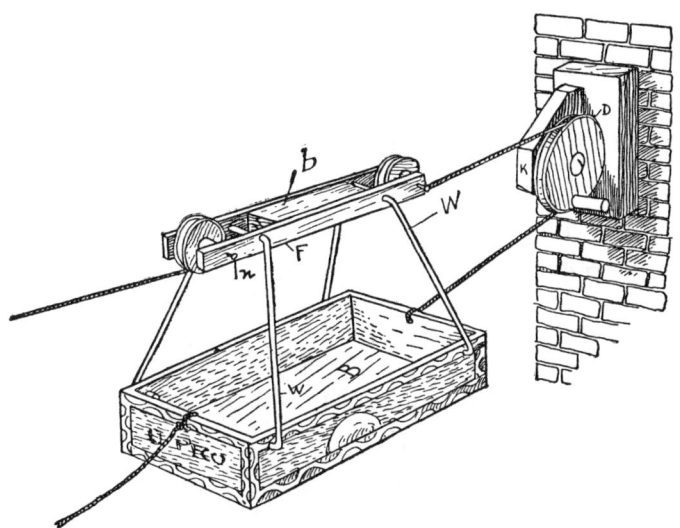

Thus, as the cord travels, the car will be pulled along, the pulleys rolling over the cord, which will also move under them in an opposite direction.

The speed of the car will depend on the speed with which you turn the crank and the size of the end pulley.

I will leave the dimensions entirely to the maker, as all cigar boxes are not the same size, but you can easily figure out the size required by the material you have at hand.

The pulleys are made from sections sawed off a curtain pole. First bore a hole through the center, — a quarter-inch hole. Then saw off a section half an inch wide, marking it carefully beforehand, so that you will be sure and get it straight.

Put these sections in a vise and, with a three-cornered file, file a groove all the way around the rim, making it fairly deep and as even in depth as possible. The deeper it is, within the side limits, the less your wheels will be likely to run off the track.

This done, fit wooden axles into the central holes, making them a tight fit and about an inch long. Into the ends of these drive pins or small brads, shown at n for the spindles, taking care that they are exactly in the center and that the wheels run true when they are all in place.

For the sidepiece of the frame F cut sticks about as long as the cigar box and separate

AN AIR-LINE RAILWAY

them by a wooden block b, a little wider than the length of the wooden axles in the wheels. Then punch holes in the sidepieces and fit the brads n of the pulleys through holes bored so that they come exactly opposite and both pairs parallel. This mounts the wheels, and forms the upper part or "truck" of our car.

The supporting wires are bent, as shown in the small sketch, and fitted through holes in the truck frame sides F as shown. These wires are a little heavier than baled hay wire. The wires fasten to the box too simply to need explanation.

The driving pulleys are cut from half-inch wood, the circles being cut roughly with a saw and then laid out flat on a board and trimmed down true to the line you have drawn with a compass, a sharp knife being used. A small hole is bored in the center of this, through which a screw spindle will fit, fastening into the bracket piece K, seen next to the pulley at the left. This piece is nailed to the baseboard D you see attached to the wall.

The pulley is grooved in the same way as the small one, with a three-cornered file. The crank handle is a spool with the flanges trimmed off, fastened to the pulley side by a screw through its center.

The drawing shows clearly how the line is strung, and the length over which you can operate it depends only on the strength of the cord you have at hand.

A Side-hill Railway

THE air-line railway just described can be used for a cash carrier in connection with your toy scales and cash register in your toy store, or can be used for a regular air-line railway outdoors, running from house to house.

After you have made this air-line railway, it will be very easy to work out the next idea, which is somewhat similar. But this railway runs up and down the side hill or the dirt bank out in the vacant lot, where you are playing at fulfilling an excavating contract or digging a cellar for a toy house. The car itself needs almost no explanation after your experience at making the upper part of the air-line railway. This frame for the wheels, shown in *Figure 3*, is exactly like the one you have just built.

This car too will run on a wire or string L, only in this case the string runs at quite an angle up a side hill and is stretched between a stake driven in the ground at the bottom and a framework at the top, shown in *Figure 2* at *F*. You will need to string the main line *L* before you can determine just how to make this car. The frame at the top, as in *Figure 2*,

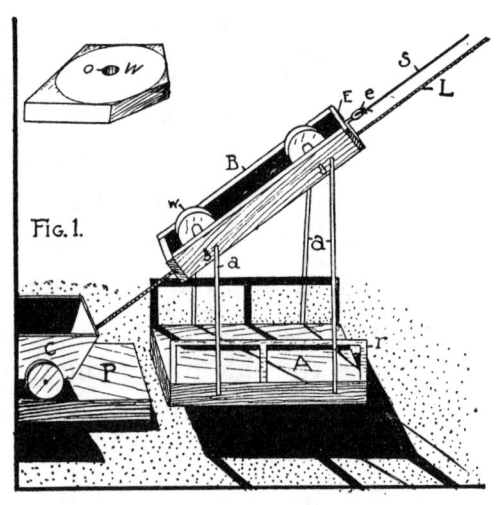

Fig. 1.

consists of two sticks *F* and a piece of inch board *P* nailed together with some short strips *f* in the shape of a letter A as shown. The board *P* should be four or five inches wide and about a foot long, while the pieces *F* should be about two inches longer. The pieces *F* are connected at their upper end by a crosspiece *D*, to the center of which the

A SIDE-HILL RAILWAY

line *L* is fastened, running down-hill to tie to a stick at the bottom. All of this framework can be held in place by nailing it to stakes driven into the ground, or the sidepieces *f* can be cut to go down below the board *P* into the ground, forming stakes to hold the frame in position, as shown by dotted lines.

Fig. 2.

At the left, in the small sketch in *Figure 2*, you can see how to take a spool *H*, fit a hardwood axle *h* through the central hole, and fix a crank *K* on its outer end.

This axle and spool is mounted on the sticks *F* at *K*, as shown in *Figure 2*, and a thread or string which winds around *H* will fasten to our car to haul it up and down.

When you have driven the stakes and fastened the upper framework in position, you can stretch the line to the stake at the bottom of the hill ten or fifteen feet away and find out the angle for your car.

The car itself, shown in *Figure 1* to the best advantage, consists of an inch board A about four inches wide and eight or ten inches long, connected to the wheel frame by small wires a. These wires are of such a length that when the wheels are resting on the wire L the car A is perfectly horizontal. It will take a little experimenting to get this just right, but the drawing shows very clearly how it is done. The railing on either side of the board A is cut of tin or heavy cardboard and is nailed in place, as shown.

Figure 1 shows the lower platform P on the wrong side of the car. It should be placed on the right-hand side under the wire L, although a platform at the bottom is not really necessary for the toy excavating car C — which may be made like the dump car previously described — to run on and off.

The small upper sketch in *Figure 1* shows how

A SIDE-HILL RAILWAY

the wheels *W* can be cut of cracker-box wood. First, after marking, the hole *O* is bored with a quarter-inch or $\frac{5}{16}$-inch bit. Then the circle, which you have drawn outside, is cut out by laying the block flat on the bench and

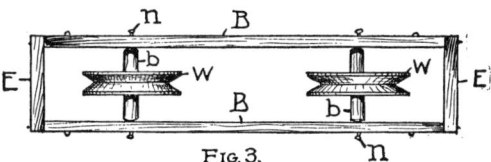

FIG. 3.

trimming down with a knife as you would slice bread, taking off corner after corner until there are no corners left, and you have cut clear down to the line. You can then take a three-cornered file and make a V-groove in the rim of the wheel as shown. The axles *b* are driven into place, and the wheels finally pivoted by the needles or small nails *n*, *Figure 3*.

This toy is great fun in a vacant lot and can be varied to suit the ingenuity of each individual maker.

If you use the toy dump car already described, you will have to make the side-hill railway platforms larger. If you want to use the small size, you can make the small car *C* out of a pasteboard box with wire axles and with wheels cut from cork. The axles can be hairpins and run right through the body of the box.

Toy Scales

IT is as natural for boys to want to make things as it is for girls to play with dolls,—a thing the boy abhors. Nearly every man, if he just thinks back a little, can remember how he made, or tried to make, something when he was a boy. Whether he ever finished it or not, the memory of the work is one of a good time.

A description of something to make is more interesting to a boy than any story, — so long as the thing he is reading about is something that will go.

Ever play store? Ever run a real store? A sand store or a lemonade stand? Of course you have, and it is fun too.

I remember a store like that some of us youngsters fixed up when I was a boy. This one was a butcher shop and put up in the empty haymow of the barn.

We fashioned great butchers' cleavers from shingles and siding, with which we cut Hamburg and made sausages, and made long wooden knives, of murderous size and outline, that were used to cut up "steaks" from the biggest potatoes we could find in the bin.

For a chopping block we used chunks of wood from the woodpile, and we weighed out our sales carefully on homemade balances.

Of tin we fashioned a butcher's saw. Our money — made from paper rubbed over a coin with a pencil — was sent up to the cashier by a real cash carrier running on a wire. That was before the days when cash registers were known to us, or I suppose we would have had one of them.

But the scales were the thing, and lucky was the one whose turn it came to keep store and who could weigh out the purchases. For the benefit of those boys who like to play store, I'm going to tell about those scales.

By making them with a steel spring instead of the rubber band and taking a little care with the bearings, these could be made fairly accurate and graduated with real weights from the grocery store; but for our toy store any unit of weight will do.

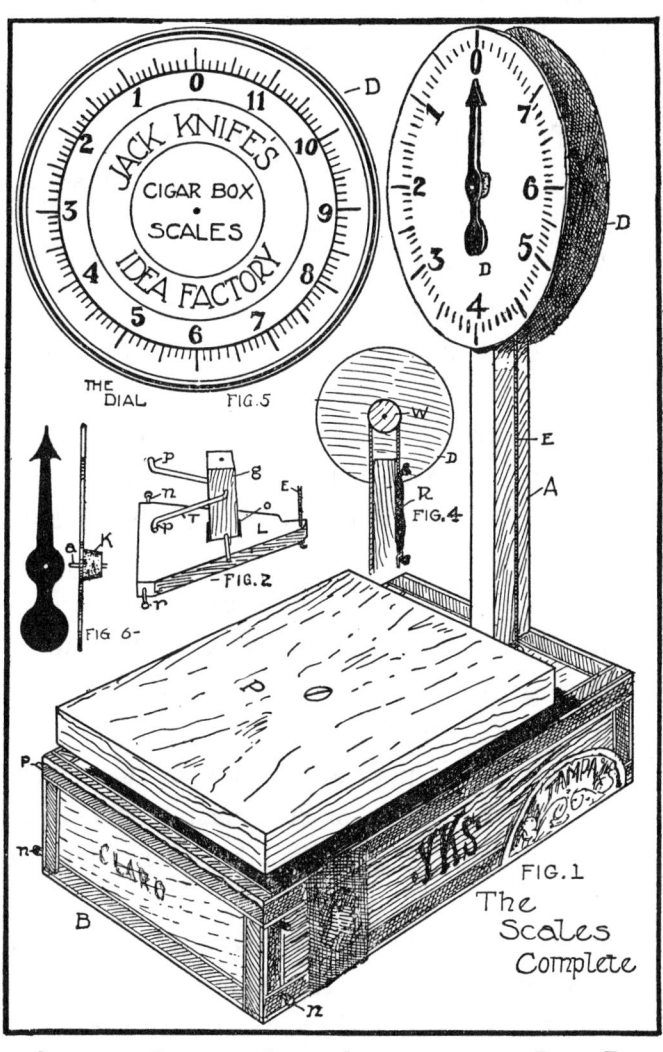

COMPLETED CIGAR-BOX SCALES SHOWING HOW THE PARTS FIT TOGETHER

The completed scales are shown in *Figure 1*. The box part below, as you can see, is a cigar box. The platform *P* is a piece of inch wood, cut to shape and fastened to an inch-square post *g* as in *Figures 2* and *3*.

This post is held by a three-cornered wooden piece *L* below, and is pivoted to it at *m*. Above, the post *g* is steered straight by a wire lever *T*.

Both *T* and *L* are pivoted to the sides of the cigar box inside at the left — the wire *T* by the little bent parts *p* and the lever *L* by brads *n*.

The right-hand end of the lever *L* goes clear to the right-hand end of the box in the middle; and at, or to one side of, its end a post *A* rises as in *Figure 3*.

On top of this post and fastened in place, as shown, are two dials of stiff pasteboard or tin with a wheel or large spool between them, as at *W*.

On the shaft of this spool are the hands *H*, one on either end, so the weight can be read from either side, and these turn with the spool.

Now from the end of the lever *L* down in

TOY SCALES

the box a string runs up and around the wheel *W*, ending in a stout rubber band on the other side and fastened as shown in *Figure 4* at *R*.

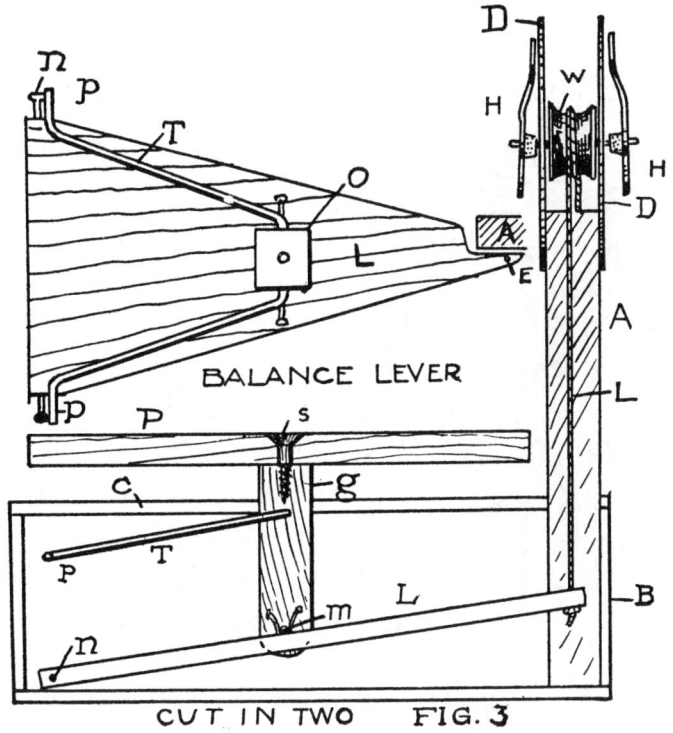

CUT IN TWO   FIG. 3

This rubber should be just tight enough to hold up the weight of the platform *P* and the levers below, so that the levers will be as high as they can go when the hand on the dial is straight up and down, or at zero.

You can see now how the scales work.

If you put any weight on the platform *P*, it will push the lever *L* down and pull the string *E* that connects *L* with the rubber band after passing around the spool *W*.

This pull on the string will stretch the band and, as the band stretches and the string pulls, the spool *W* will turn and thus turn the hand on the dial.

The string will pull until the weight on the platform balances the pull of the rubber. By looking at the dial then and seeing where the hand points, you can show your cus-

TOY SCALES

tomer "two pounds" or "two pounds and a half" with as much pride as the real storekeeper.

The parts of the scales, now that we know how they work, are not hard to make.

The wire for T is ordinary baled hay wire or the like. The platform P is fastened to the stick or post g by a single flat-headed screw.

g is joined to L below by the joint indicated in *Figure 2*, which shows a wire or brad m, *Figure 3*, running through a hole near the bottom of g, which, in turn, is sticking through a hole in L — a loose fit.

Thus the wire and the brad m act as the axle or pivot, and a couple of pins or brads on either side, as shown, will keep it from sliding out of place.

The size and dimensions I must leave to you, for they will depend on the size of your cigar box.

The wheel W above can be cut from an old curtain rod or you can use a large spool.

Make the stick or post A thick enough so that the dials will be far enough apart to permit the spool to fit loosely between them.

Plug up the hole in the center of the spool, drive darning needles in the exact centers, and slip your dials, which have been cut as directed from heavy pasteboard or tin, over the needles by means of small holes in the centers of the dials.

If you like you can enlarge on a piece of paper the dial in the illustration and use it, pasting it on the tin or pasteboard.

The hand or pointers are glued to small pieces of cork and slipped over the ends of the darning needles after the dials are nailed in position on top of the post A. The pattern for the hands is shown separate, *Figure 6*.

The rest is easy. You can leave the cover on the box or not, as you see fit, by cutting holes for the posts A and g and fitting it on in halves.

A Toy Cash Register

AFTER you have finished making the toy scales, you probably will want a cash register to record the amount of the sale. It is not hard to make a model cash register, as shown in the drawing, planned of a size so that the drawer of the cash register is a cigar box.

The cigar box that you pick out for the drawer will be the basis of all your measurements, but when the toy is done, it will look like *Figure 1*.

This is a toy which was made by a boy acquaintance of mine and which worked exceptionally well.

In appearance the cash register is as shown in *Figure 1*, but the details of the mechanism are shown in the other drawings. *Figure 2* perhaps shows best how the toy cash register works.

There are six keys to this register, and these are made of ordinary pants buttons wired on to the end of a wooden lever *L*, cut of cigar-box wood. All of these levers are arranged in a row, pivoting on a wire *W* with about one-

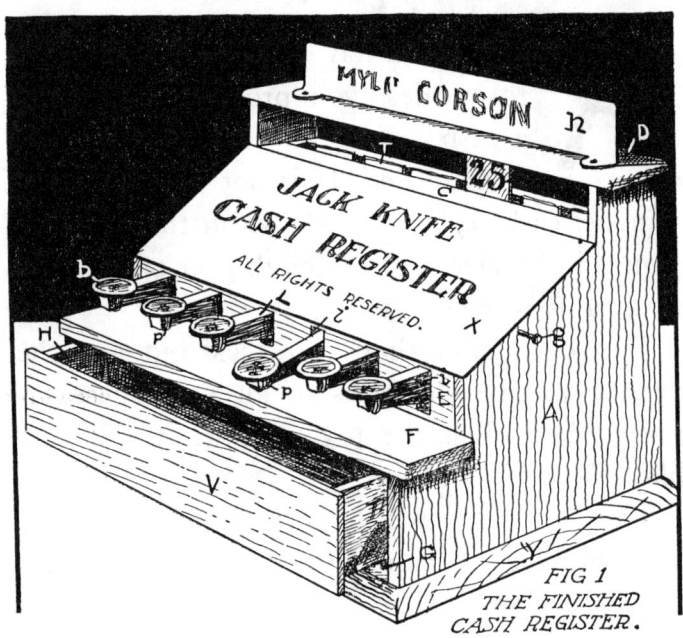

FIG 1
THE FINISHED CASH REGISTER.

fourth of the length outside the box part of the cash register. At the end of each lever inside is a tin piece *T* with a number on both faces. This tin is arranged below an opening in the wooden piece *C*, so that when the key *b* is pressed down, the other end of the lever

A TOY CASH REGISTER

goes up, and the tin piece *T* is exposed with its number, as shown in *Figure 1*.

The drawer *H* slides in just under this row of levers, running on blocks *G* in the corners to hold it a little way above the floor of the register. Across the top of the row of levers inside the box is a flat piece of cigar-box wood *K* about two inches wide, or thereabouts, slanting as shown, and pivoted to end pieces *A* by the small nails *n* shown in *Figure 3*. You can see that whenever one of the levers is pressed it will lift up on the lower end of this piece *K*, causing it to turn around the nails *n* as a pivot.

At the right-hand end of the piece *K*, as shown at *J* in *Figure 3*, is a small wooden catch pivoted on a nail *d*, driven into the edge of *K*. This piece *J* is guided between blocks *N* nailed to the side pieces of the cash register case *A*. The catch *J* drops into a notch *P* in the edge of the drawer as shown in *Figure 3*. The lower part of the piece *J* is slanted, as shown, so that when the drawer is pushed into place, *J* is lifted and drops into the notch *P*, holding the drawer in place.

Figure 4 shows how a rubber band is arranged between small nails under the drawer to act as a spring and shove the drawer out whenever it is released. Two nails *m* are driven in the baseboard several inches apart while the nail *a* is driven into the bottom of the drawer. The nails *m* are toward the front of the case, while the nail *a* is at the back edge of the drawer. Thus, when the drawer is pushed in, the nail *a* catches on a rubber band stretched between the base nails *m* and pulls it back. When the drawer is clear in, the catch *J* holds it shut. A piece of wood *V*, *Figure 2*, as large as the front end of the case, is nailed to the front edge of the cigar box as shown, to keep the drawer from going too far in.

Now if you press one of the keys, you can see how the drawer will fly out, for when you press down on *b* in *Figure 2*, the lever *L* pushes up on *K*, no matter what button you may push. This lifts the catch *J* out from the notch *P* so that the rubber band is free to throw the drawer open, which it does. A little stop is nailed on the back of the slot piece *E*, *Figure 6*, so the drawer cannot fly too far out. This gives you the entire principle of a cash register,

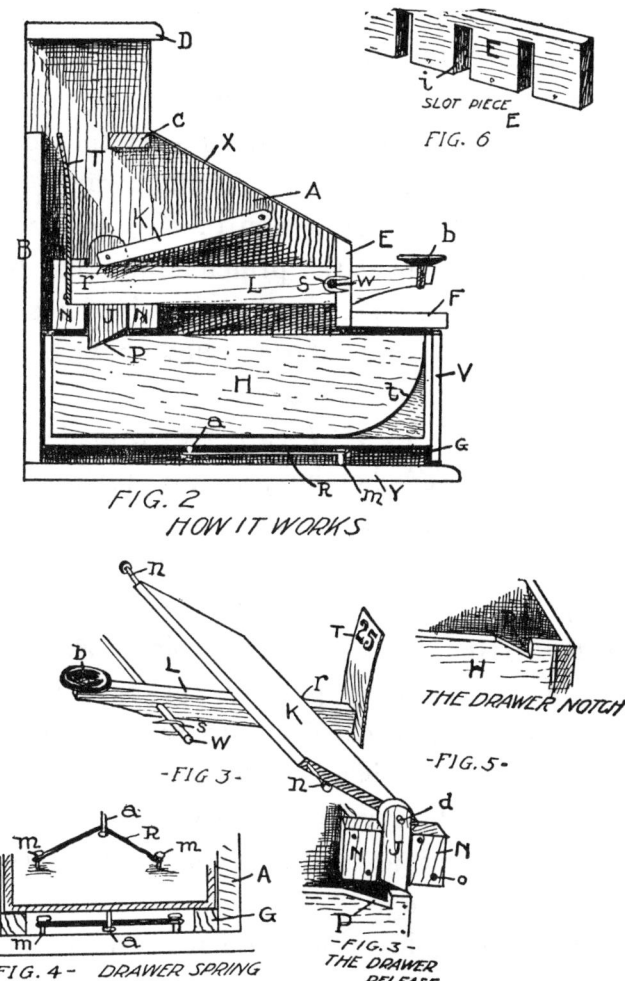

CASH REGISTER. DETAILS OF THE MAKING

for the number plates *T* are numbered 1, 5, 10, 25, 50, and 100, and whenever you press the button opposite, this number is shown above, while at the same time the drawer flies open. By a little ingenuity you could arrange also to ring a bell by the action of *K*, if you wish.

Having explained the principle and also having shown the shapes of the pieces in the drawing, little else is necessary in describing how to make the toy cash register.

The end pieces *A*, *Figure 1*, are made from wood from a cracker box, as are also the shelf *F* in the first notch of the side pieces, the slot piece *E* in front of this notch, the strip *C* in the position shown at the top, and the piece *D* on the extreme top of the side pieces *A*.

Over the slanting part of the cash register frame is a tin piece *X* cut to fit and fastened in place with brads or small nails. Fasten this temporarily, however, as you will need to take this off to get at the mechanism if anything should go wrong.

With these directions, the rest will be easy.

A Telephone Line

DID you ever make a tin can telephone?

Simply take two empty tin cans and punch a hole in the center of the bottom of each. Run a string through the holes and tie a button or a large knot inside so the string can't slip out again.

Let the string be, say fifty feet long, and let a boy at each end hold the can in his hands, drawing the string tight.

If nothing touches the string — be sure you don't have your fingers on the bottom of the can — when a boy talks in the can at one end, you can hear him at the other, and I'll tell you why.

When you talk into the can, if you hold your fingers lightly on the bottom of it, you'll feel it shake or vibrate against your finger tips.

If a string then runs to another can some distance away, and you start the bottom of your can shaking or vibrating by talking into it, the string will carry the vibrations to the can at the other end, provided you keep the string tight, this will reproduce your words just as you spoke them into the first can, only not quite so loud.

This kind of a telephone is called an "acoustic" telephone and can be made to work up to a distance of several blocks if you construct your line carefully and make a "diaphragm," as it is called, — and which corresponds to the bottom of the can, — a little more sensitive to the voice, so it will vibrate harder when you talk into it. Anybody can understand how the telephone is going to work now.

In the first place, get two boxes about the size you want for your phones at each end. Cigar boxes will do very well.

In the bottom of the cigar box, and about in the center up and down, cut with your knife — after first marking it out with a compass to be sure it is true and round — a circle an inch less in diameter than the bottom of the box is wide.

Just opposite this hole and in the cover cut a circular hole two inches in diameter, or

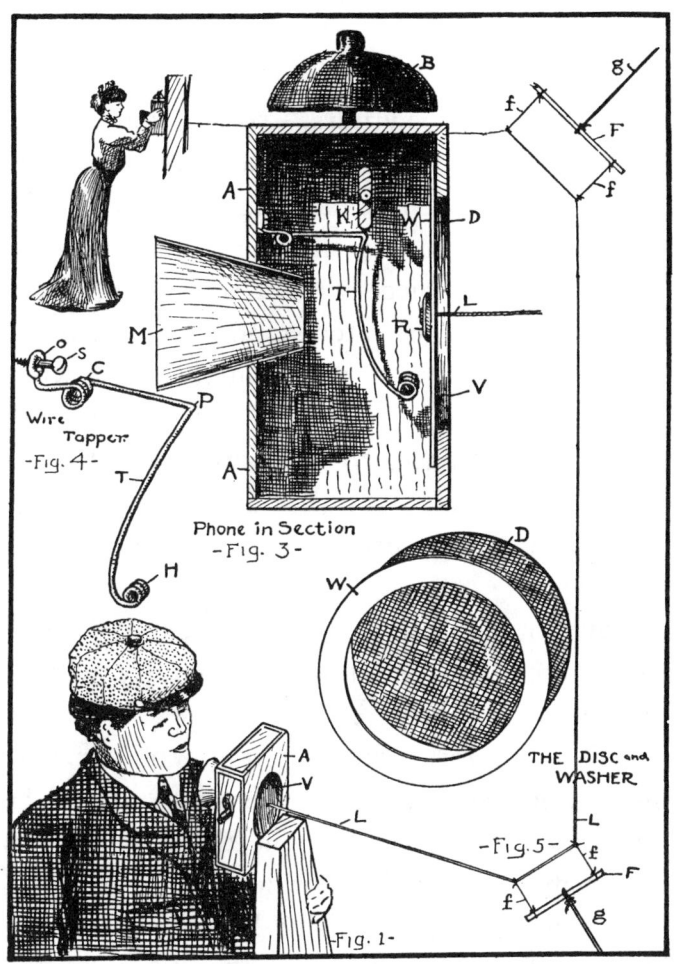

DETAILS OF CALL TELEPHONE MADE FROM A CIGAR BOX

thereabouts. This hole will be for the mouthpiece to fit into.

Take a piece of light but tough paper, such as is used in typewriters, — or, if your line is to be long, stout Manila paper will do, — and cut from it a circle as l rge across as the bottom of your box inside.

Dampen this piece with a wet cloth, — not wet enough so the water stands on the surface too much, but good and damp, — and while still in this condition, glue it or stick it with strong library paste to the bottom of the box inside and over the large round hole that you cut there, being sure that it is even around the edges.

Never mind stretching it, for as it dries it will stretch itself, and when fully dry will be taut as a drumhead.

This is to form the diaphragm of our telephone and, as you can well imagine, it will be much more sensitive than the thick tin bottom of a tomato or baking-powder can.

If your line is especially long, you can use instead of paper, which might not stand the pull of the stretched line, a circle of "tintype

A TELEPHONE LINE

tin" such as photographers use for tintypes. It may be obtained from almost any photographer.

The mouthpiece, *Figure 2*, is cut out of tin or stiff cardboard like the pattern, and when bent up and curled into a conical shape as

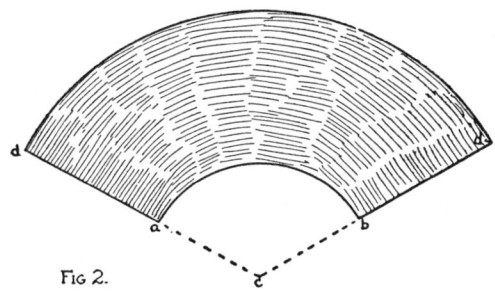

FIG 2.

at *M*, *Figure 3*, fits into the hole in the cover of the box with its smaller opening pointing toward the center of the diaphragm *D*.

To further hold the diaphragm in place, a washer *W* is glued or pasted over the edge of the paper, the outside diameter being the size of the paper diaphragm and the inside the size of the hole in the bottom of the box over which the diaphragm fits.

This finishes the telephone proper, and the line is ready to be strung.

Fasten two of these phones up in their desired places, held out from the wall by little blocks so that the diaphragm, when pulled by the line *L*, won't touch the wall, as in *Figure 1*.

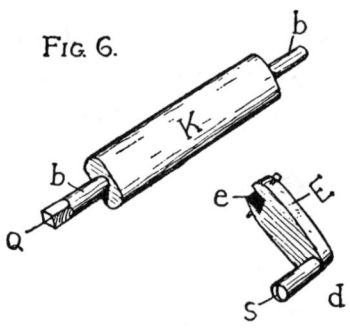

FIG. 6.

An inch hole is bored through the wall and the string prevented from touching its sides by the little threads shown in the separate sketch at *f*, *Figure 7*, held by tacks.

Where the line needs support outside, it cannot be tied to anything, but may be held by little threads or insulators *h* as shown in *Figure 8*. Corners are turned, as in the corner sketches, *Figure 5*, by means of threads *f* from a light stick *F*, held in turn at its middle to some support by a cord *g*.

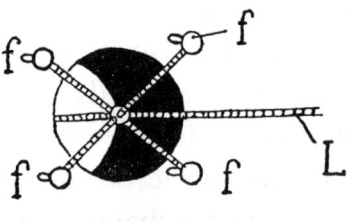

FIG. 7.

The string is fastened to the diaphragm at

A TELEPHONE LINE

each end by means of a flat button *R* so it won't pull back through.

The hole in the center of the diaphragm must be as small as possible.

When you are sure your line is tight and that nothing is touching it to hinder its vibration, talk into the mouthpiece at one end, and your partner at the other end can hear you plainly.

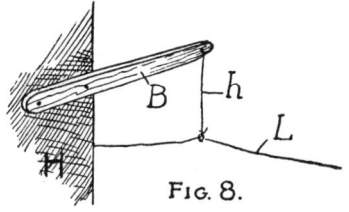

FIG. 8.

To call up your partner, all you have to do is to tap sharply on the diaphragm, and in the drawings I have shown a way to do this with a crank.

Toward the top of the box a piece *K*, *Figure 3*, runs crosswise, pivoted on a shaft *b* cut on it. This may be made of one piece of wood, as indicated in Figure 6, or the shaft may be separate. A crank is on the outer end.

Inside, a wire "tapper" bent up, as shown in *Figure 4*, with a spring part *C*, a corner to press on *K* at *P*, and a hammer or head *H*, is fastened to the box in the position shown by a small screw *S* through the cover and a small block if necessary.

When the wire is in position, it pushes upward on *K* when the flat side is toward it or down, and then the hammer below barely touches the paper diaphragm.

When you start to turn the crank, the wire corner *P* will be pressed down more and more as you turn, until it will suddenly run off of *K* and by its spring fly back and up. This brings the hammer below sharply back against the diaphragm, and the boy at the other end hears a sharp tap, twice for every turn of the crank. The tapper, however, does not interfere with the working of the phone after the boy is called up.

You may use a stout hemp shoe thread for the line *L*, if it isn't over a block long. A longer line needs thin wire.

Fix this line up between your shop and the house kitchen or shed, where they will be more likely to let you bore a hole through the wall, and then maybe your mother can call you to dinner easier. Perhaps if you promised ahead of time that you would come right away, she would let you bore the hole anyhow.

A TELEPHONE LINE

Another kind of call arrangement for this type of telephone is shown in *Figure 9*. This shows the telephone part made of a doughnut of inch wood, instead of a cigar box as at *A*, but with a paper diaphragm, etc., just like the phone we have described. This phone has the mouthpiece *M* cut into the wood itself rather than made separately of paper, the central part being an inch hole.

This phone is fastened to a lath *L* but separated from it by little blocks *m* so the diaphragm will not touch the lath. There is a hole in this lath

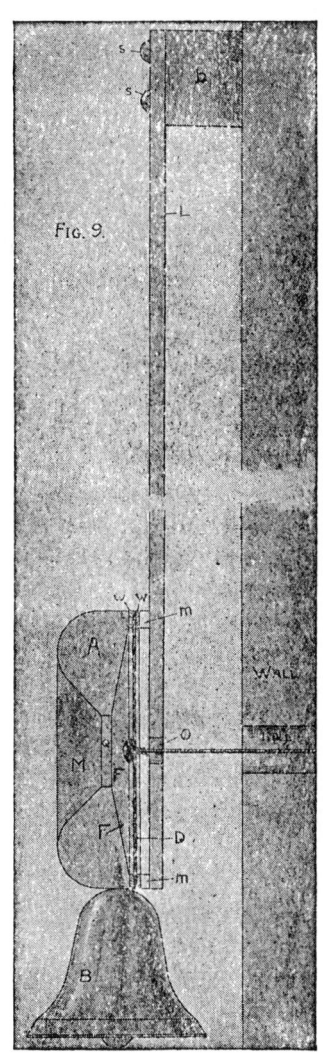

Fig. 9.

81

also at *O*, through which the line passes. The lath is fastened by screws *S* to a block *b* at its top end, so the lath itself acts as a wooden spring to keep the line tight. An ordinary bell *B* is fastened to the phone at the bottom by a small screw. Both ends of the line are the same, and you can easily see how this arrangement works, for if you take hold of the bell or lath at one end and shake it back and forth, the action of the string line will shake the lath at the other end and ring the bell, thus calling the other party.

This kind of telephone is great fun and is very practical where only two parties are concerned and the line is not over a block long.

A Toy Phonograph

HERE is a toy phonograph that will actually play real music, and you will also have the fun of making it yourself in your own workshop. You will have to buy the records and the needles, but all the other material you can pick up.

If you look at one of the hard rubber records, you will find that one spiral line is cut into the disk, starting at the center of the record and running to the outside. Examine this line closely, and you will see that it is not a straight but a wavy line. You may have to take a reading glass or a microscope to see the waves, but in most records you can see them quite plainly.

On the machine a needle follows this line as the plate turns, so that the needle moves back and forth, just as the record guides it. This wiggles the lever to which the needle N is fastened above, and that in turn causes the diaphragm b to vibrate.

When this thin membrane, called the diaphragm, shakes or vibrates, it makes the air vibrate just as the voice or the orchestra player that made the record did, so that from the

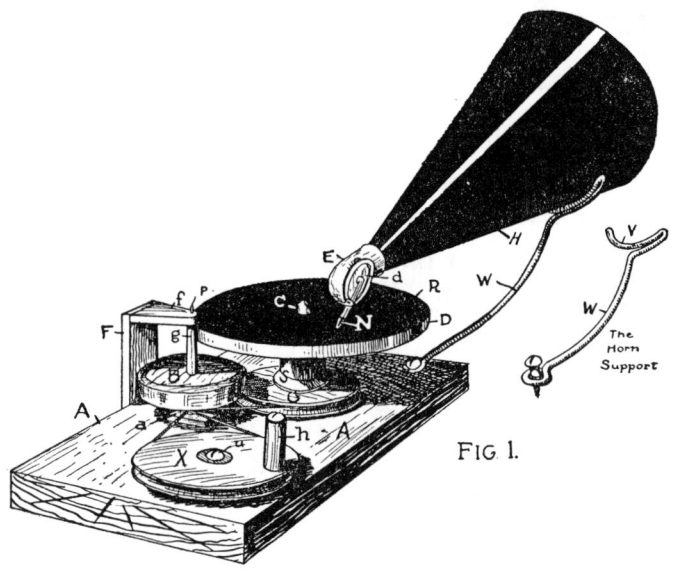

FIG. 1.

diaphragm comes the sound of the voice or music sent out through the horn *H*.

Having this part explained, all the rest of the machine you need to understand is the part that turns the record or disk. That you can easily see from the drawings.

The record is shown at *R* supported on a

A TOY PHONOGRAPH

wooden table or wheel disk *D*. This in turn is fastened to a spool *S*, which has at its bottom a pulley *O* fastened so that when this pulley turns, the record above is turned, all rotating about a stick or a shaft running up through the hole in the spool.

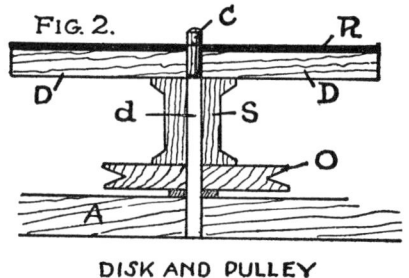

DISK AND PULLEY

Off to one side is a flywheel *B*. You can probably find somewhere a small iron wheel and save the bother of making a wooden one.

This wheel is mounted on a shaft, as shown in *Figure 4*, having two pulleys — small ones — at its lower end, one of them level with the pulley *O* we have already fixed.

From the second pulley on this flywheel shaft a belt runs to a third and large drive pulley at *X*, *Figure 1*. This is arranged on the level of its pulley on *g* by putting washers under it between the base and the wheel. The wheel *O* should have at least one washer under it to keep the wheel from rubbing on the baseboard when it turns.

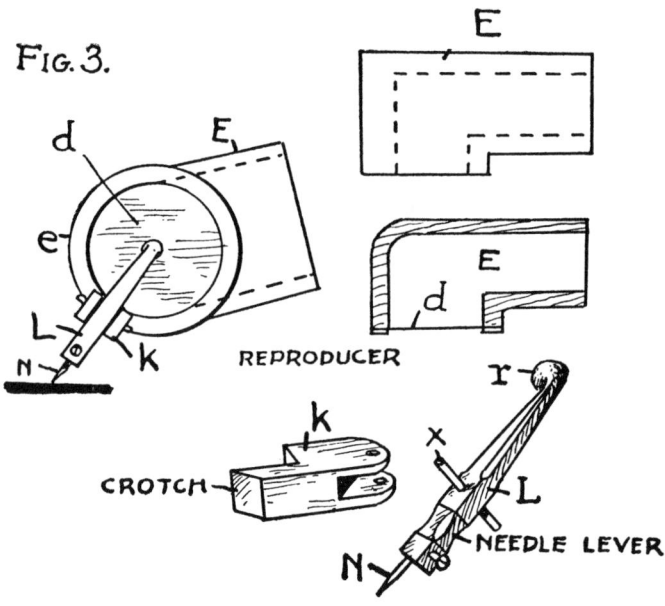

FIG. 3.

REPRODUCER

CROTCH

NEEDLE LEVER

On *X* a handle *h* is mounted. Thus, you see, when the handle is worked to turn *X*, this turns the flywheel at a high rate of speed. The belt from this turns *O*, and thus the record is revolved.

A TOY PHONOGRAPH

In playing, when you make *O* turn ever so little faster, the music will jump up a key, and if you run it slower it drops down a key. The flywheel is to enable you to turn the disk at an even speed.

The wheels *O* and *X* are about three inches in diameter, and the heavier the better. The pulley on the shaft *g* below, shown at *P* in *Figure 4*, should not be more than three-quarters of an inch in diameter.

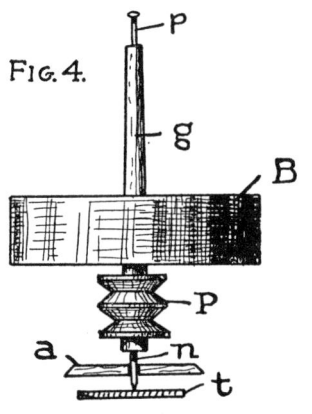
FIG. 4.
– BALANCE WHEEL –

The shaft *g* is mounted in the frame *F, f, Figure 1*, between bearings made of needles, *Figure 4*, the lower needle from the lower end of *g* passing through a hole in a small stick *a*, fastened to the base *A*, with its end resting and pivoting on a piece of tin or glass *t*. This is shown in the sketch of the "balance wheel."

How the disk and pulley are fixed is also shown in the separate sketch, *Figure 2*, and you can see in this the washer between O and A. The shaft d in this sketch is loose, so the spool S can turn freely about it. The short piece C above is tight and turns with D.

Now for the reproducer E, *Figure 3*. This is cut from a block of pine about two inches square on one end and two and a half or three inches long. Bore inch holes in this piece, as in the dotted line drawing, making one hole from the center of one end to within half an inch of the other, and then boring another to meet it at right angles, leaving a rim at least a quarter of an inch wide all around.

With a knife and wood-file trim and smooth this piece off until the hole is clean and smooth inside and the outside round. At the surface of the side hole fasten the diaphragm d as shown.

This diaphragm d may be a piece of thin writing paper, dampened and fastened on with glue. Or better, it may be a thin strip of mica or isinglass. Glue will fasten these too, and then glue a pasteboard washer a quarter of an inch wide on top of that, as at e.

The lever L is shaped, as shown, from a

A TOY PHONOGRAPH

piece of hardwood and fastened to pivot loosely on a wire or brad X, in a wooden crotch K, glued to the side of the reproducer in the position shown.

For the points buy a paper of loud victrola needles. The length from the tip of the needle to the center of the diaphragm, — the other end of the lever, — is about twice the length from the center of the diaphragm to the wire X. That is, the wire X should be midway between the needle end and the diaphragm center. I once made a talking machine with a reproducer six inches in diameter, using a piece of tin tacked on the side for the diaphragm, and a pine lever. It worked as well as any other I have tried, but was too big and cumbersome.

A bit of candle wax or glue will fasten the lever end to the center of the diaphragm. The needle N fits into a tiny hole in the lever end made with a brad driven in and pulled out again, and is held in place by a tiny screw at the side, procured from some jeweler's scrap heap.

If the paper diaphragm is put on dampened,

when it is dry you will find it as tight as a drumhead. The horn may be of tin or pasteboard, funnel-shaped of course, and fitted into *E* at its small end. You can easily figure out the pattern by making one of a newspaper or a bit of wrapping paper first, and then copying it with the material you want to use.

The horn is held in place by a wire holder *W* bent into a loop at one end for the screw to go through to hold it to the base, and into a sort of "Y" at the upper end as at *V* for the horn to rest on.

The base can be made of a cigar box, which provides an admirable sounding-board.

A Writing Telegraph

NO doubt some of those who read this article saw at the St. Louis Fair the wonderful electric writing telegraph, or "Telautograph," as it is called.

Here a man sat at a desk with a pencil and wrote and drew pictures, while above him, on another piece of paper in a separate machine, a pencil guided itself in the same manner and drew the same lines. It was very interesting, especially when one thought of writing from one city to another, as can be done with this machine.

Having seen the instrument at the Fair, as a boy, I set to work to devise one for myself when I returned home. At first I had trouble, but finally I hit upon the simple scheme of the apparatus shown in the drawings. This is really surprisingly easy to make. The principle is very simple also.

You see, in the first place, the pencil P is

held in a wooden arm or lever *A*, and this wooden arm is pivoted on a screw eye *S* at about the middle. At the outer end of this arm or lever a string *L* fastens and runs to

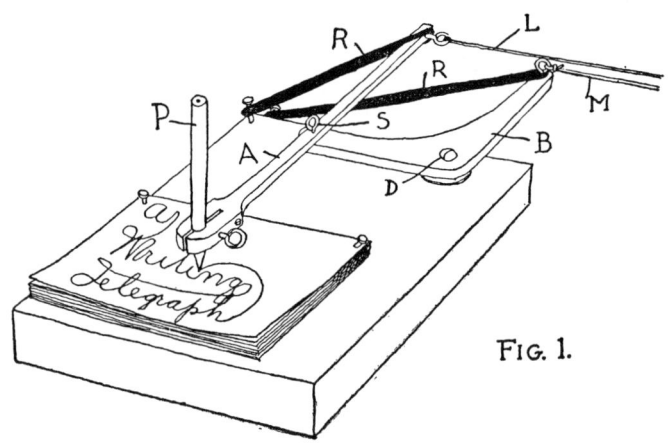

Fig. 1.

the other end of the line to a similar lever, while rubber bands *R* at either end keep this string tight. You can see from this how, if you swing the pencil sideways so as to move this lever about its pivot *S*, that the pencil at the other end will slide sideways back and forth in exactly the same way as you move this first pencil. This string *L* therefore carries all the side motions of the pencil.

A WRITING TELEGRAPH

The pivot S, however, fastens to the end of a bell crank B, made of wood and having arms at right angles of equal length pivoting on a screw D at the corner of the bell crank. From the outer arm of this bell crank — which, by the way, lies parallel with the first lever arm holding the pencil — runs a string M to a similar bell crank on the instrument at the other end of the line.

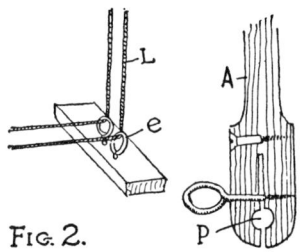

FIG. 2.

Now if you move the pencil up and down, this moves the second arm of the bell crank right and left, and pulls or pushes the string M. Rubber bands R keep this tight as before, so that any up-and-down motion of the pencil P through the moving of this bell crank transmits up-and-down motion to the pencil at the other end of the line, and any up-and-down motion at one end carries exactly the same at the other end. We therefore have an instrument which produces two motions: right and left carried by the string L, and up-and-down carried by the string M, so that between the two strings any combination of writing motions — up and down, horizontal, circular, or slanting — are transmitted and written at

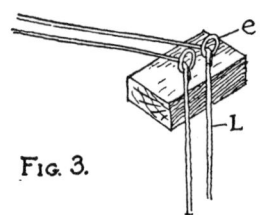

Fig. 3.

the other end of the line. This makes a wonderful writing telegraph, and one from which you can get a great deal of amusement.

This toy is very simple to make. The base is nothing but a piece of inch wood, about eight by ten inches or even larger. The first lever *A* is made of half-inch wood. Near one end a hole is bored the size of the lead pencil you are going to use, and a saw cut is made down through the hole and extending a little distance back, as in *Figure 2*. A small hole is drilled through one side just back of the pencil and extending as far as the saw cut. By screwing a screw eye through this hole to the wood on the opposite side, the pencil is clamped tightly on the end of the lever and can be held at any height from the paper. A small wood screw farther back at the end of the saw cut will prevent the wood from splitting. Back of this the lever may be cut

A WRITING TELEGRAPH

down so that it is not over a half an inch square.

The bell crank is made of thin cigar-box wood with each arm half as long as the first lever A. In other words the distance from the screw eye S at the center of the lever A to the screw D at the corner of the bell crank is equal to the distance from S to the pencil P on the other lever. In mounting the levers and bell crank, be sure the bearings work freely with little friction; under the bell crank B — and between it and the baseboard — a washer is fitted around the screw D to keep the bell crank from rubbing on the board.

The strings which form the line are ordinary hemp shoe thread and can be fastened to holes in the levers or to screw eyes, — the latter making a neater looking job. It is very easy to see how the rubber bands are fastened to keep the strings of the line always tight. The instrument should be adjusted so that when it is at rest the arms and bell crank are in the positions you see.

The writing pad is nothing but a little penny tablet that you can tack on the board, and a small pencil can be put in the proper location so that the pencil can reach all parts of the board.

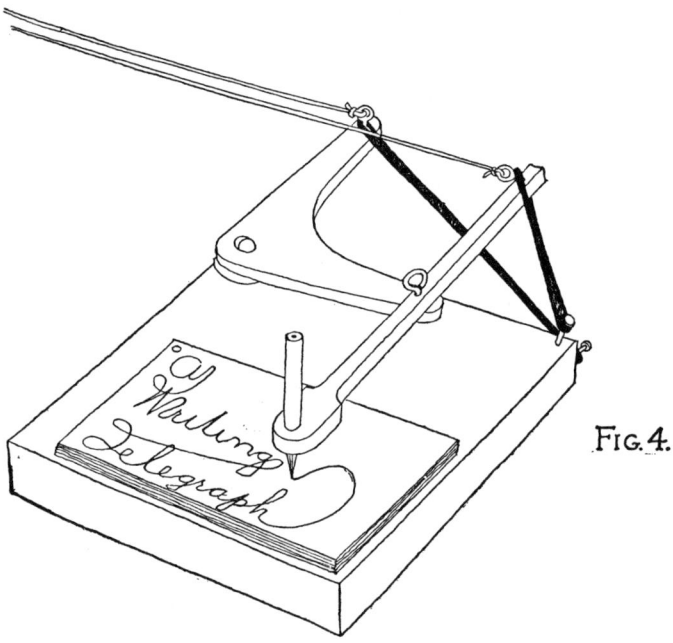

Fig. 4.

In connecting the instruments, run a string from the straight lever to the same location on the other instrument, while the bell cranks are connected by a separate string *M*. If the instruments are identical, with the bell cranks on the same side, they will write exactly alike;

A WRITING TELEGRAPH

but if they are on opposite sides, — as shown in my sketch here, — then the one instrument will write upside down.

If you want the line to turn a corner, you can run the string through screw eyes or a little block of wood screwed into the wall, as shown in *Figure 3*. If you want to run the line upwards, you can run the strings through the screw eyes as shown in *Figure 2*, having a similar connection at the top end of the line, which may carry the strings in through the window to the table on which the other instrument is set.

The rest of the toy is so simple that it needs no further instruction than the drawings.

A Toy Crane

THERE is no end to the toys and useful articles that can be made from ordinary cigar boxes of various sizes, the number and variety being limited only by the ingenuity of the maker. One of the simplest is a model of a crane such as is used for loading ships.

Along the English docks one sees many of these perched on top of a towerlike arrangement on wheels, the track on which the wheels run stretching the length of the dock edge.

Along this track the towers move, driven by water power mostly, until they come to the part of the ship where they are to work, and there they stop by the hatchway.

A man in the crane house on top of the tower works the levers, and the big steel boom swings out over the ship's hatch, drops a rope down into the hold, then at a signal hauls up

A TOY CRANE

until there comes into view the load of trunks, or boxes, or freight of some kind at the other end of the rope.

Stopping the pull on the rope, the driver pulls another lever, and the house on top of the tower begins to turn, the boom turning with it, so that the load on the end of the rope swings over and away from the ship, till it is stopped over the dock.

Then the driver lets the rope slip and down goes the load onto the dock, to be loosed by a "navvy" below.

To set the load further away, the boom is dropped lower; by hauling it in nearer and straighter up and down, the load can be brought closer to the tower, so that the crane can set it down or pick it up anywhere within the range of the length of the boom B and for the entire length of the track on which the tower runs.

Instead of a wheeled car, the one I show slides on tracks, but wheels can be easily made from half spools, if you prefer that kind.

Our toy will be worked by hand, of course, but if you have a toy motor or engine, I have no doubt many boys are ingenious enough to make one to work with power.

The box part *A*, *Figure 2*, is made with a space *x* cut out forward, as I shall explain

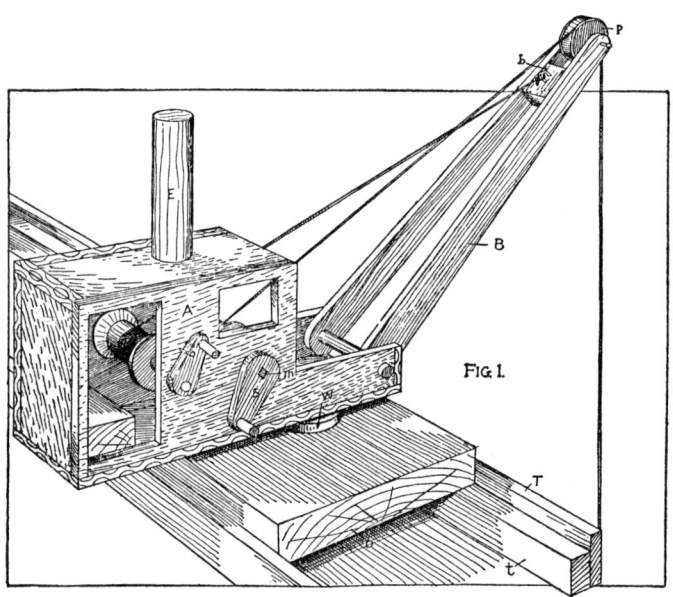

FIG. 1.

later, and in this space the boom *B* made of two sticks with a pulley at the top is fixed.

Back in the box are two spool windlasses on which the "ropes" or strings wind up. These are turned by cranks, as at *C* outside, and the string from each has its own work.

A TOY CRANE

One string fastens to the boom, as shown, so that when its spool is turned by the crank, thus winding up the cord, the boom is lifted, or lowered by turning the crank in the opposite direction. The other string goes over the pulley, so that turning this crank raises or lowers the weight on the end of the main rope.

The turning of the whole apparatus is done by hand, though it might be done by turning a third crank near by.

For the "cab" part, select a good-sized cigar box, shaped as shown, and out of the corner saw the part x shown in the detail of *Figure 2*.

In doing this watch out for nails, or you will dull your saw. This done, smooth off the edges, and with a sharp knife cut the windows and door.

Having selected the spools for the windlasses, fit their axles tightly in place, leaving one end m long. Make the holes in the cigar box and fit the axles by driving them through the spool inside the box.

The way of making the crank is shown in *Figure 2*, using cigar-box wood, shaped as

BOY'S BOOK OF MECHANICAL MODELS

shown; one can also make it of wire. Another way is shown in the larger drawing of the complete machine.

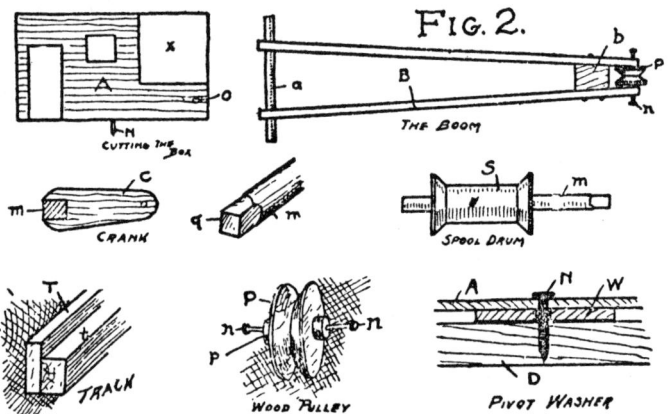

Make the boom as at *B* in *Figure 2*, the block *b* fitting up at the top and the small pulley *p* fitted between the outer ends. The sketches show how to make the pulley from a piece of curtain pole or round wood.

Have the boom about twice as long as the cigar box, and pivot it at the open end of the "cab" part as shown, the stick *a* being the pivot for its turning. The car is a block of inch wood, and to this the "cab" is pivoted, as in the detailed drawing in *Figure 2*. Here

A TOY CRANE

A is the cigar-box bottom, *N* the pivoting nail, *W* a thick wooden or pasteboard washer, and *D* the board "car."

By fitting the pasteboard washer, and smearing it generously with lard, you will have a crane turning easily so you can swing your loads quickly. Lard may also be used on the track if you want the "car" to slide smoothly.

The making of the track is simple; the lath *T* is merely nailed up against the square stick *t*. The whole arrangement can be built along the edge of your workbench.

Before calling the toy done, test the bearing of the pulley to see that it runs easily and that the nails *n* which drive into the ends of the wooden axle *p* to form the pivots are centered right. Also see that the cranks are not so long as to hit each other in turning.

If the holes happen to come too near, you can fix one crank on one side of the box and one on the other. For the "rope" use ordinary hemp cord.

A Toy Trip Hammer

HERE is a real noise maker! Turn the crank and the four hammers — you can have more if you want to — will beat a continuous tattoo on the anvil stick L. There are four beats for every turn of the crank, and the noise of each hammer depends on the speed of the drop. If you want a big noise, add rubber band springs as at R above to make the hammers come down harder.

It is no trick at all to make this toy, as everything about it is easy to procure and there is nothing hard to cut out. You need to be careful and get the ends of the lever arms A at the right place next to the stick axle S, so the paddles or "cam" sticks will hit them right. While there are a number of parts to make, so many of them are duplicated that after all there is not much work to the making.

A TOY TRIP HAMMER

To understand how it works, look at the small drawing. Here the square wooden shaft is shown at S with the wheel W fastened at the far end. By making this wheel W grooved, you can run the hammers with a water motor, steam engine, or toy electric motor. The crank k can be put on the side of the wheel too, if you wish, and thus run it in this way.

On the square sides of the stick shaft S are four small wooden paddles or cams P, all the same length, which stick out beyond the edge of the square shaft as shown. They are spaced at equal distances along the shaft, as in the big sketch, and each is on a different side.

In front of the shaft, and about opposite the center of the wooden shaft S is a wire pivot or shaft a, on which the lever arm A for the hammers will pivot. This wire is supported from beneath by a wooden bracing piece F which has notches cut where the levers come, as in the upper sketch, where the levers A are shown in section. The square notches in F are seen just beneath.

The levers A are fixed so that the short end comes almost up to the shaft S opposite the paddles, and the pivot *a* should be a couple of inches away at least, depending on the length of the paddle pieces *P*.

The other ends of the levers are at least twice as long as the short end and even longer will be better, ordinarily. At the outer end are the hammers. These are square blocks of hard wood, or, if the hammer toy is small, round sections of broomstick can be used. Under the hammers the stick *L* is fastened to the baseboard on which the hammers hit.

Now turn the crank in the direction of the arrow and see what happens. One of the paddles *P* as it turns will come in contact with a lever arm *A* and push down on this end. This raises the hammer on the other end from its anvil and stretches the rubber band *R* if this is fitted.

As the shaft continues to turn, the paddle *P* runs off the lower end of the arm *A*, leaving it free, so that the rubber or its own weight brings it down with a bang. No sooner is this down than the next hammer goes up and bangs down, then the next and the next; and by this time, the first paddle having come around

A TOY TRIP HAMMER

again, the first hammer starts the process all over again.

In making this toy use a piece of inch-square wood for the shaft, say eleven inches

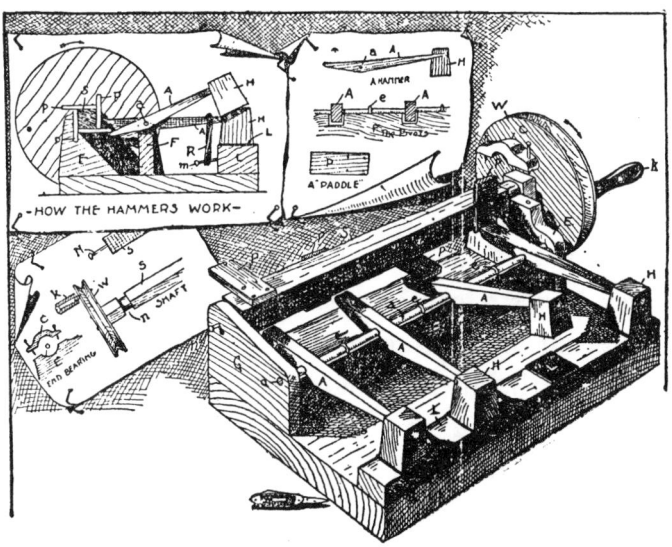

long. Space the paddles two inches apart, with the one on the left an inch from the stick end, and you will have a nice size to work on.

Make the paddles of cigar-box wood, or thinner, and let each one stick out three quarters of an inch beyond the stick edge. Fasten them on securely.

The levers *A* can be made, say nine inches long, with the short end two inches long from the end to the shaft *a*.

The base can best be made of a cigar box, but can be of wood of a size to fit the parts already made. Cut the shaft bearings as shown.

The big end bearing is shown in a small drawing and with the cap removed in the big drawing and is cut of half-inch wood, the top being flat, and with half of the circle in it. Over it fits a cap *C* with the other half of the circle cut in it as shown.

Make the piece *E* large enough so the hole for the wire *a* can be made in it as shown. Make the other bearing piece from the same pattern, but without the cap, and get the hole for *a* in the right place. Instead of the cap scheme for *G*, a nail *n* is fitted loosely through a hole in *G* and driven into the end of the square shaft *S*.

Measure the right distance and fasten these bearing supports to the baseboard, then hold the shaft *S* in place with the end against *G* and mark where the bearing *C* comes at the

A TOY TRIP HAMMER

other end. Cut the stick down round with your knife, being sure to get the rounded part in the center, until it fits in the bearing cut for it, when the cap C is nailed on and does not bind.

Make the piece F of half-inch wood, as high as the wire, and cut notches in it for the levers A opposite each paddle P. Cut out the levers and fit the hammers as shown, then make holes for a and slip the levers loosely on the wire as you put it in place, fitting the levers into notches.

The piece F is fastened in place by small nails in through the end pieces G and E. It should be just high enough to support the wire a. Small wire staples e will hold the wire in place.

Cut the hammers from a square stick, boring a quarter-inch hole through them for the lever arms A to stick in, the stick pieces being rounded to fit tightly into these holes. Glue can be used also to hold them.

If you do not want noise, put a leather piece under each hammer on top of the stick L, but make L high enough so the hammers will strike it squarely when they come down. If rubbers are fitted for springs, stretch them from the stick *A* to a nail *m* in the back of the anvil stick *L* as shown.

The way of making the crank and the pulley wheel *W* is shown separately also, and anything not plain from the description is easily seen from the drawing.

But, after you get it all done, don't blame me if mother won't let you run it in the house.

An X-ray Machine

STEP up, ladies and gentlemen! Step up! Here you see the greatest wonder of the century! The X-rays, the X-rays! You can see right through your hand, through a board, through this thick city directory," and the "spieler" held up a thick volume to enforce his remarks.

It was at a county fair, and the voice of the "spieler" sounded loud above the steady hum of the voices around and the cries of the other men who were offering their wares near by.

I, a small boy, elbowed my way through the crowd and stood finally where I could see clearly.

"Step up, ladies and gentlemen! Step up! The wonder of the ages! Only ten cents a look! See through your hand! See through a book! See through a board! Only ten cents!"

A young man stepped up and handed the

man ten cents, then stooped and looked into the eyepiece of the machine. The man pressed a button, and a little one-candle-power electric light with a green globe lighted up at the other end of the machine.

There were two tubes supported on pedestals at their middle, and one looked through the length of one tube into the end and through the length of the other, — or so it seemed.

"What do you see?" asked the man, so the crowd could hear.

"A greenish light," said the young fellow.

The man took up a piece of board and placed it between the tubes so that in order to see the lamp now, one must look through the board.

"What do you see now?" he shouted.

"Same old thing," was the answer.

"Look! Look!" shouted the man. "He sees through the board."

But my attention was riveted on the machine, and now I understood. The "spieler" noticed my attention.

"Come on up, sonny," he said, waving his long hand my way and beckoning me on.

AN X-RAY MACHINE

"Come on and see through this book," and he held it up again.

"Aw, no," I said. (I was only a small boy.) "Why, you do it with looking-gla— No, I guess I can see through that without paying ten cents."

"How's that?" asked the man, but in a subdued voice, and he was off his stand in a minute and by my side.

"Here you, sonny," he said, taking me by the shoulder. "You get out of this and right smart."

I "got," but I carried the secret of the machine with me, nevertheless. It was nothing but an arrangement of looking-glasses or mirrors, and in the drawings I have shown how you may very easily make one for yourself.

Cigar boxes may be had at any cigar store for the asking, so get five of these to start with, all the same size if possible, so as to simplify your fitting work.

Across the bottom of two of the boxes and in the middle, mark off two lines crosswise of the box and as far apart as the end of the adjoining box is wide. Then saw out the space between the lines and take out this piece of the box bottom.

—Fig. 1—
THE FINISHED MACHINE

One of these places is shown at *a*, where *A* joins *B*, *Figure 1*, and the other at *e*, where *D* fits into the bottom of *E*.

The boxes *B* and *D* have the upper end knocked out entirely and at the other end have a piece of the side near the bottom taken out which is as wide as the end of the box *C*, which will fit into it. These places are shown

AN X-RAY MACHINE

at *b* and *c*, *Figure 1*. *C*, of course, has both ends knocked out.

By fixing the boxes in this way, you can see that there will be a continuous passage from one to the other.

Open the cover of *A* and *E*, and inside, just over the hole into *B*, fix at an angle a piece of looking-glass which has been cut to the right size and shape. The best way is to fit a piece of pasteboard in place and have the glass cut from it.

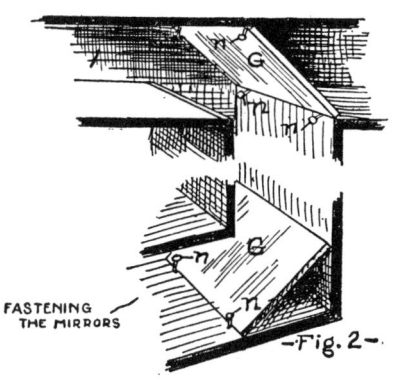
FASTENING THE MIRRORS
—Fig. 2—

Figure 2 shows how the glasses *G* are fastened in place with brads or tacks *n*.

Another mirror goes into the corner of *B*, below and opposite the hole into *C*, fastened also with tacks. The boxes *D* and *E* are fixed the same way. You can test the boxes as you go along by looking through them to see if you have the right angles to the glasses.

BOY'S BOOK OF MECHANICAL MODELS

Cut two eye holes in the upper boxes *A* and *E* at *O* at each end, *Figure 3*, round but not too large — say half an inch. Fasten the box covers down. Fasten the boxes together at

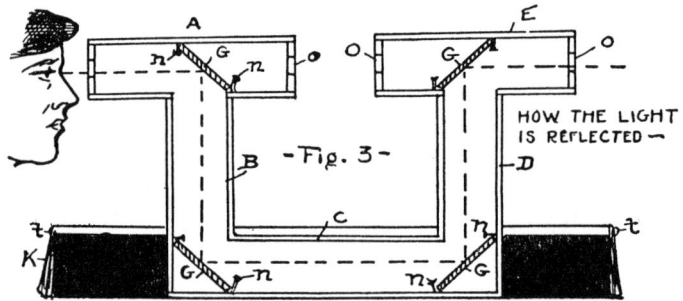

the joints with glue, further strengthening the apparatus by gluing strips of cloth or heavy paper over all the joints and cracks where light might get through.

As to the baseboard, it may be fastened to the bottom box, as in *Figure 1*, or above the bottom box, as in *Figure 3*. The latter way is better, as it hides some of the machine that gives away the working of it, but that necessitates cutting a hole in the board for the bottom part to fit into. When nailed in place, a curtain *K* of cloth will hide the lower box.

And now you can see by the dotted line in

AN X-RAY MACHINE

Figure 3 that if you look in one end, pointing the machine toward the window or light, the eye will see in the line shown dotted, and if you put your

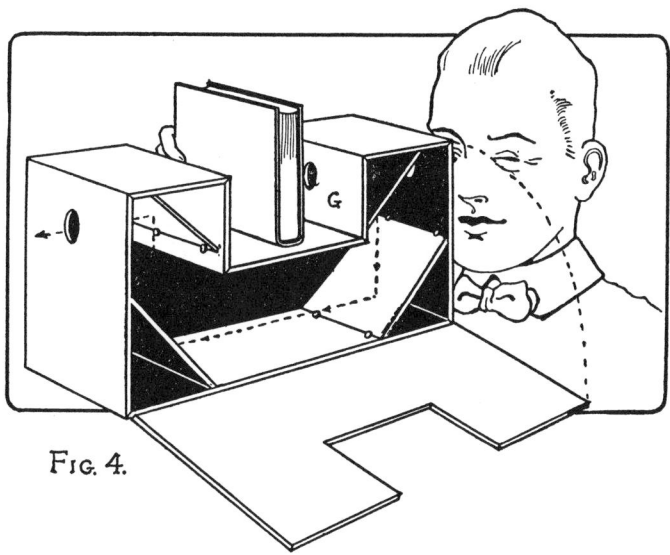

FIG. 4.

hand, or a board, or a directory, between the boxes *A* and *E* as in the picture at *L,* you can see right through it — or think you do.

If you have not enough cigar boxes to make this large X-ray machine to look through with both eyes, you can easily make one out of a single cigar-box to look through with one eye, as shown in *Figures 4* and *5.*

BOY'S BOOK OF MECHANICAL MODELS

Figure 4 shows the completed X-ray machine with a side — the cover of the box — folded down, and the dotted line through the box shows the travel of the boy's sight in looking through the machine. This is also shown in *Figure 5*.

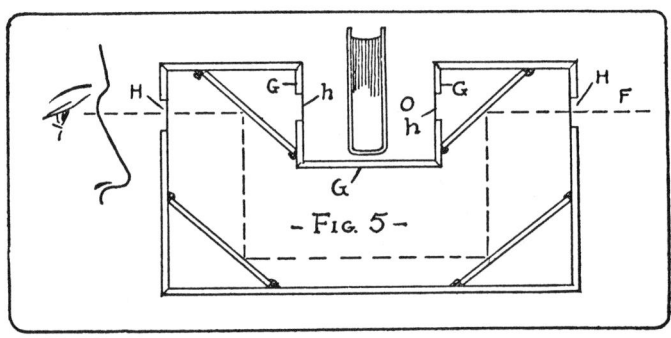

As to directions, proceed as follows. Get a nice clean cigar box of the thin kind, — not too thin, but about two inches deep. Set this box on your bench with one of the long sides up and divide this side into three parts. Saw out the central part as deep as half the depth of the cigar box, as shown at *O* in this sketch.

Next take some cigar-box wood and line this notch *O* so that the sides are continuous, as at *G* in *Figure 4*. This work you will have

AN X-RAY MACHINE

to do with the sides of the box removed, as in *Figure 4*.

Figure 1 shows the scheme in perspective with the side taken off, and also shows the well or gap in the side of the box which we have just made.

Next make the holes *H H h h*, seen in *Figure 5*. Only two are seen in *Figure 4*, the other two being hidden.

You can take a sharp bit and bore through from one end to be sure the holes are in line, or you can burn the holes through with a hot poker. The cut hole is better, but you will have to blacken the edges.

Now you can shut the lid, hold this up to the light, and look through all four holes in the box. If you put your hand in the notch *O* where the book is shown and then look, you can't see through, and you have not as yet an X-ray box.

The next step is to paint the inside of the box, lid and all, with shoeblacking or black paint without gloss. "Dead black" is what you want, and a ten-cent can will go a long way. This has to be put on the inside so there will be no reflections in the mirror of the inside of the box. Be sure too that all joints in the box are light-tight, like a camera.

The next step is to insert the mirrors. These you can cut from an old broken looking glass, if you have a ten-cent glass cutter, and they should be as wide as the inside of the box and just about square. Be careful not to scratch the glass, or it will show when you look through.

Mount the mirrors in place inside the box, as shown in *Figure 5;* they should be at 45-degree angles in the corners of the box, as shown, and are held in place as indicated in *Figure 5*.

You can test the angle of these mirrors as you fit them by shutting the lid of the box and looking through the hole at *H*. This will show you when they are all in place, if you look straight through, as by the dotted line, and out the further hole *H*, without looking through the holes *h h* at all.

At first fasten the glass loosely until you are sure of the angles, but when these are right, drive the tacks down as firmly as pos-

AN X-RAY MACHINE

sible without straining the glass, so there will be no rattle nor distortion from changing angles.

Now you can shut the box up and nail down the lid, and after this is done paste paper strips over the joints and around the corners to keep light out. Then you can paint the whole outside as you wish.

The next thing is to hand it to your friends for use. You can show them how to look through their hands, or put a book or board in the notch between the sight holes, as in *Figure 5*. There is a lot of fun to be had with this toy.

A Shadow Picturescope

BETWEEN the fun you have in cutting out the pictures, blacking and pasting them up, — as I shall direct, — into "shadow pictures" or "transparencies," and the added fun you have looking at them afterwards through the view-box or scope, this simply made toy should furnish a good many hours' amusement for the whole family.

Let us suppose you have a photograph of your house. Trace its outline on a piece of cardboard, using a piece of carbon paper (or a piece of paper which has been rubbed on the back with lead pencil) for the tracing. Trace the windows and the bare outline of the house and trees; that is all.

Now cut this out. The outline can be cut with scissors, but the openings, such as the holes among the trees in *Figure 1* and the windows, had better be cut with the point of a sharp knife.

A SHADOW PICTURESCOPE

We will make this a night scene, with all lamps in the house lighted. To get this effect, paste at the back of the window openings pieces of yellow or orange tissue paper. At

FIG. 1.

the back of the whole house and for the sky (but not over the windows) paste a piece of thin blue tissue paper, as in the dotted portion, *Figure 1*.

Now for the view-box, *Figure 2*. Select a small cigar box, as shown. Knock the bottom out and fit a square paper funnel at one side. This box, of course, should be large enough so

BOY'S BOOK OF MECHANICAL MODELS

that the picture you have made can be seen through it. You will see what I mean as I proceed with my description.

This funnel is made as in the pattern *Figure 3*. The lengths of the parts are as follows: —

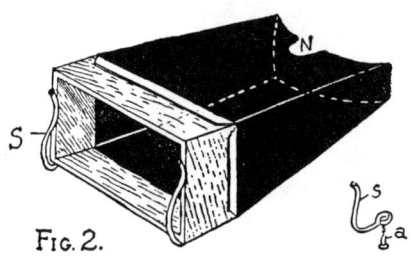

Fig. 2.

The funnel is about six inches long (*E* to *F*). From *A* to *B* (and the distance from *C* to *D* is the same) is as long as the box you have selected is long outside. *B* to *C* and *D* to *E* equal the height of the box outside, so that when bent around square, this end will fit snug around on the outside of the box end. The flaps *f* are left so that the funnel can be pasted on the box, and *g* is to be pasted to the edge *F–E*, when the pattern is bent on the dotted lines.

G–F is about an inch and a half high, as is *H–K*, while *L–K* and *H–G* are four and a half

A SHADOW PICTURESCOPE

inches long and curved a little. The line shown in my drawing has a notch N cut to fit the nose of a person looking through the scope.

Little wire hooks, such as S, are fastened to the front of the box, as shown, to hold our picture.

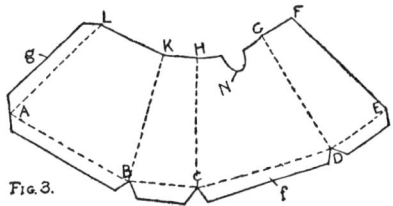
Fig. 3.

Now paste a pasteboard frame around the house shadow picture, this frame being of a size to fit the front of the box in its outside measurements and to fit your picture in its inside dimensions.

Punch pinholes in the blue tissue sky for stars. Slip the picture in between the box front and the clips S, hold the box to the light, and look through the small end of the funnel; you will be surprised at the result.

This is only one picture. You can make scores more by cutting out pictures of buildings, fountains, animals, and people, and mounting them on transparent tissue paper backgrounds of colors to suit sky, grass, or anything else. A railway train at night would make a fine picture, with the windows shining yellow, a dark blue sky above, and all beneath black.

A Model Grain Elevator

YOU boys who are making toys that operate along the same lines as their larger prototypes will no doubt be interested in this plan of a model grain elevator. Some day you may own a large one, and then your knowledge of the construction of these simple but faithful models will perhaps serve you to good purpose.

Figure 1 shows the model complete. *Figure 2* gives a view of the toy with a side removed. *Figure 3* shows details of the belt conveyor and buckets. Annexed to *Figure 3* are some of the other details of the making. How the toy works is shown in *Figure 2*, where you can see the parts better.

First, grain — or its play substitute, sawdust — is put into the hopper G, *Figure 2*, below at one end of the elevator. When you turn the crank H, *Figure 1*, outside the building, the belt B, *Figure 3*, between the two

BOY'S BOOK OF MECHANICAL MODELS

spool pulleys travels along. This belt has tin buckets *D* fastened to it, so that when these come down they scoop up some of the "grain,"

carry it up, and dump it as the bucket goes over the pulley at the top.

In dumping, the "grain" drops into the top bin, filling it up ready to be drawn out of a spout *T, Figure 6*, into your waiting "wagons" at the other side.

A MODEL GRAIN ELEVATOR

For material select a cigar box, or for a large model pieces of thin wood from the sides of a cracker box or the like, some inch pieces for the heavier parts, and for the base a couple

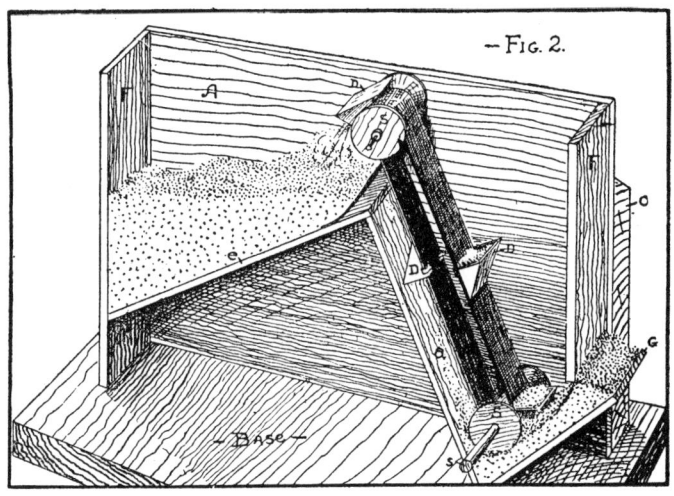

of good-sized spools of the same size, some tape for the belt, and some tin for the buckets. We will make a big model.

Cut end pieces F of thin wood, as wide as the spools are long or a trifle wider. They can be any convenient height to suit your elevator, but a foot high is not too much. Fit sides to these also of thin wood, and nail one side on as in *Figure 2*, making as good a job of it as you can.

Plane off a roof piece *B*, as shown in *Figure 1*, slanting it off from the center line and letting it overhang a quarter of an inch all the way around. Nail this in place carefully. Next fit in the pieces *a* and *e*, arranging them as shown in *Figure 2* to leave plenty of room for the spools *S S* in their proper places.

Cut a piece out of *F* at the right-hand end and fit in a slanting board *G* for the hopper. You can fit a tin or cardboard at either side of this if you wish to keep the "grain" from spilling out sideways when you pour it into the hopper.

Fit the spools onto tight wooden axles, as in *Figure 5*, the lower one with the axle sticking out several inches at one end and the other end cut off nearly flush with the spool end. Drive pins or brads *n* into the ends of these wooden axles for spindles. These will fit through bradawl holes in the wooden sides of the building, the nails turning in the holes. Be careful to get the axles of the spools parallel to each other so the belt will not tend to run off.

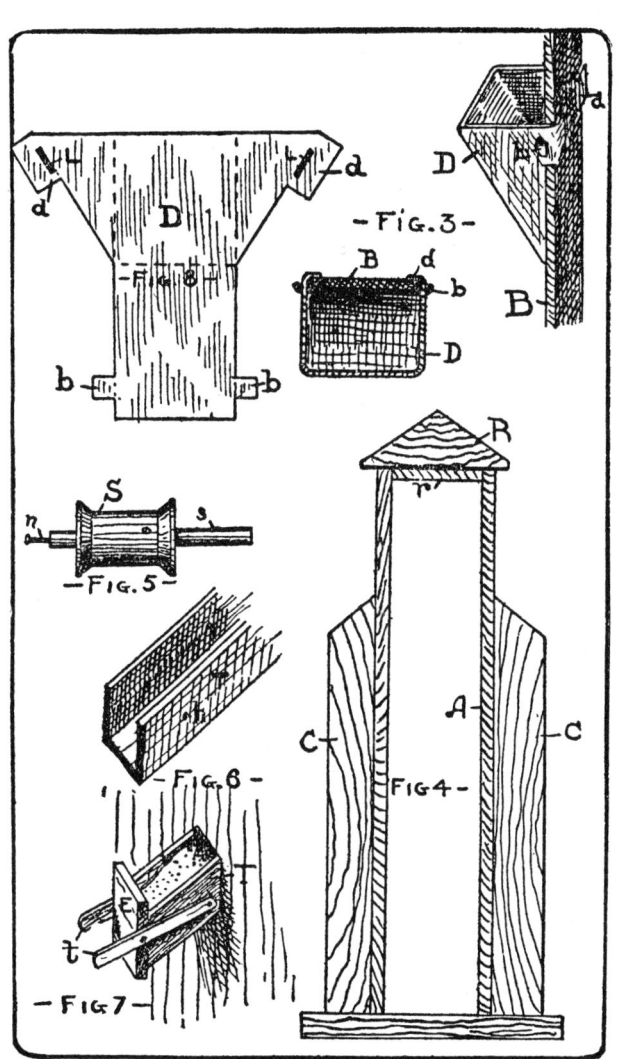

Fit the spools in a location allowing room enough for the buckets without their hitting at top or bottom or against the slanting board *a* as they pass and dump above. Now to fix the belt and the tin buckets.

The belt is a strip of ordinary tape such as your mother uses in her sewing. The buckets are of tin bent up and attached to the belt as in the separate drawing, *Figure 3*. In the first place the pattern shown at the left is cut out.

This is made with the central part as wide as the tape belt. Its length is a little over twice as long as the width of this central part. The top part has a little triangular piece on either side, and a little flap *d* is left at the outer edge of this.

On the other end of the pattern are two little flaps *b* and when this much is done — and you had better cut the first pattern out of paper till you make one that suits you — fold the tin piece on the dotted lines.

Where the flaps *b* come on the flaps *d*, when the lower part folds up so they meet, punch little slots *L* for the flaps *b* to stick through.

A MODEL GRAIN ELEVATOR

This can be done with a hammer and small screwdriver.

Set the bucket as it is cut and folded, against the tape belt and bend the flaps d back around the belt, hammering them so they hold the bucket to the belt tightly without slipping. This fastening is shown in the sketch marked *Figure 3*.

Stretch the belt tight on the pulleys, sewing the joint, and then put on the other side of the building. To make the elevator more realistic, two one-inch pieces, *C C*, *Figure 1*, are fastened outside the main part of the building, extending up to within a few inches of the roof, where they are cut off slanting, as shown.

One of these is cut short to allow room for the crank pulley *P*, shown in *Figure 1*. This is a round disk of wood fastened to the spool shaft tightly and having a wooden crank *H* with which to turn the shaft. If you wish, you can groove the pulley *P* and run the elevator by your steam-engine or by water power. The whole arrangement is fastened to a baseboard to complete it.

If you have taken care to mount the spools parallel so the belt will run right, the elevator is now ready for business so far as lifting the grain to the bin is concerned.

To drain this bin when full, a trough, *T*, like *Figures 6* and *7*, is fixed slanting out to the end of the elevator, this being built of three pieces of cigar-box wood.

At the end of this trough a gate *E* is fixed, held by side pieces *t* pivoted on nail *h*. By lifting on the handle connecting these side pieces the gate *E* is lifted, and the grain flows out of the elevator bin. Drop the handle, and the gate shuts.

Model Elevators

THERE are all kinds of elevators, some for passengers, some for freight, and some for grain, but the next one I'm going to tell you about is for freight, and light freight at that. You might even call it a mail elevator, for we boys used the one we fixed up to carry notes up to the attic window from the ground outside, — so you see it is for light loads.

What you need to start in with are a few sticks of thin wood, a cigar box, and two empty tape spools. The line is of wire and string, or string alone, if you can't get the wire.

The first thing is to cut up the cigar box as you see at *A* in the drawings, *Figures 1* and *2*.

That is, merely cut the narrow sides of the box down thin to within a few inches of the end, first nailing on the bottom and cover of the box and sawing across where they end.

Of course, before you cut the box, you should

mark where you're going to cut, and then the two sides will surely be alike when you are done.

This cutting leaves, as you see, a small box at the bottom formed by what used to be one end of the cigar box, with two arms *a* sticking up, each arm an inch wide and about two-thirds the full length of the box.

Now take two tape spools, *W*, *Figure 2*, and with a three-cornered file or with your knife cut grooves around the rim. Through the hole in the center drive some tight wooden axles *b* and cut them off so that they are almost, but not quite, an inch long and stick out equally on either side.

TRYING THE MODEL ELEVATOR

MODEL ELEVATORS

Some tape spools have a very small hole in the middle. In this case you can take a quarter-inch bit and enlarge the hole if the wooden axle be too light to drive a needle *n* into without splitting it.

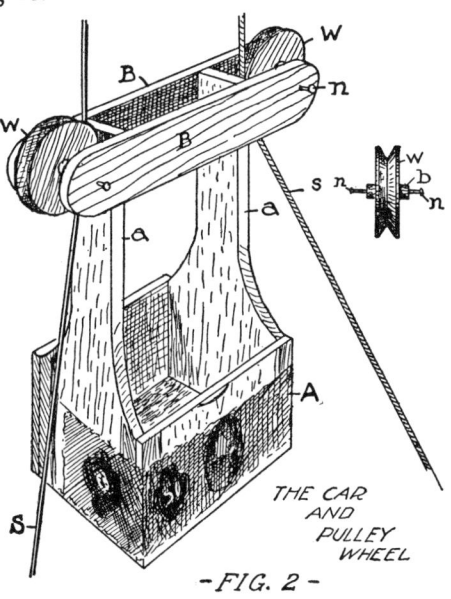

THE CAR AND PULLEY WHEEL

- FIG. 2 -

These finished, cut two pieces *B* from the odd pieces of cigar box or of other thin wood, — both alike, rounded at the ends, three quarters of an inch wide, and long enough to stick out an inch beyond the pieces *a* when put in the position shown in *Figure 2*.

The wheels are mounted, you see, by driving needles or small brads n through holes in the pieces B into the ends of the wooden axles shown at b in the little sketch of the wheel alone.

Make the holes in the pieces B first, taking care to get them opposite, and have them large enough so that the needles or brads will turn easily. Also start the needles or brads into the axle ends before you mount the wheels in the frame, just driving them in a little way and then pulling them out, so that when you come to feel around through the bearing for the exact center of the axle, the needle will easily find the hole that has already been made.

After the wheels are in place, and the needle driven home, you'll have some wheels that turn very easily and freely.

This finishes the car, and we'll start to work on the line, which is the easiest part to make. In the drawings I have shown the line running to a second-story window.

Instead of fastening the top of the line to a board D fastened crosswise, as it is in the

MODEL ELEVATORS

drawing, you may fasten the top of the line to screw eyes screwed into the top of the window frame, which will save a little work — only then the elevator won't always stop at exactly the right place.

The screw eyes E at the top should be just as far apart as the distance inside the pulley wheels W on the car, that is, a little wider than the cigar box.

The line S on the left is stovepipe wire and is stretched very tight. At the bottom it is fastened to a large stake, not directly under the left-hand screw eye, but off a little to the left and out from the house.

The line from the right-hand screw eye is a piece of stout cord which runs off to the right and around the pulley in the top of a stake F some distance away.

Before you string the lines tight, pass them through between the wheels and the pieces a of the car, so when the car runs, they'll run on the inside of the wheels.

The stake that the pulley is fastened to should be, as I said, a little to the right, but the distance depends on what you'll use your line for. A third of the height of the line is a good distance, but if you want the elevator to go up faster, make it a little less. It won't carry so much weight, though. If you want to carry heavier loads, make it a little more than a third.

After the right-hand string runs over the top of the pulley on the stake, it runs back toward the first stake at the left and ends in a stick or ring for a handle.

This is how the elevator works: Take the loose string with the ring H in the right hand like the boy in the picture *Figure 1*.

Suppose the car to be at the bottom. If you pull on the string, it will tend to stretch tight between the pulley below and the screw eye above, as in the dotted line. It can't take that position, though, because the car is in the way, and before it can, the car must move up to the top.

This is just what it does, as you'll see when you try it; and when you pull the string, up goes the car, with a speed depending on how hard and quick you pull. Go easy at first till you learn how, or you'll send the car bump

MODEL ELEVATORS

into the top stick *D* and spill your load or even break the car. A little practice will make you an expert.

This first elevator is probably the simplest that can be made and is good for distances up to the first story. It is not suitable for much of a height, however, and if you want to make one that will work up the side of the wall to the attic window, follow the directions on the crank elevator. This is almost as simple to make as the first type, is more like a real elevator than the first one described, and will lift quite a load. The elevator part can be made of a cigar box, as in *Figure 8*, so things cannot fall out.

A CRANK ELEVATOR

First take some laths, or if you can't get them, cut some sticks about an inch and a half wide from the side of a cracker box or some such thin wood.

Cut two of these sticks a little longer than your elevator car is to be wide, — a little wider than a cigar box, if you are going to use that for the car.

Arrange these two sticks edgewise on two others, as at *A* in *Figures 3* and *4*, leaving space enough between them for two spools *G* to fit easily.

These pieces *A* are fastened to the under strips *D* with brads, and the strips *D* have their other ends nailed to the under side of the window casing, as you see at the top of *Figure 3*.

One piece *D* is near the end of *A* at the left; the other is a distance off equal to a little less than the width of the box you use for the car, so that after it is nailed in place, strings or wires *L* may be let down for guides on either side of the car, running from nails *n* driven into *D*.

Before you nail the upper frame to the window casing, fix the two spools of equal length — the ones you have made to fit between the pieces *A* at *G* — as in *Figure 4*, cutting a small groove for the string around its middle, as in *Figure 5*.

Mount one spool at the right end of the pieces *A* and the other so that the string from it will hang down midway between the pieces

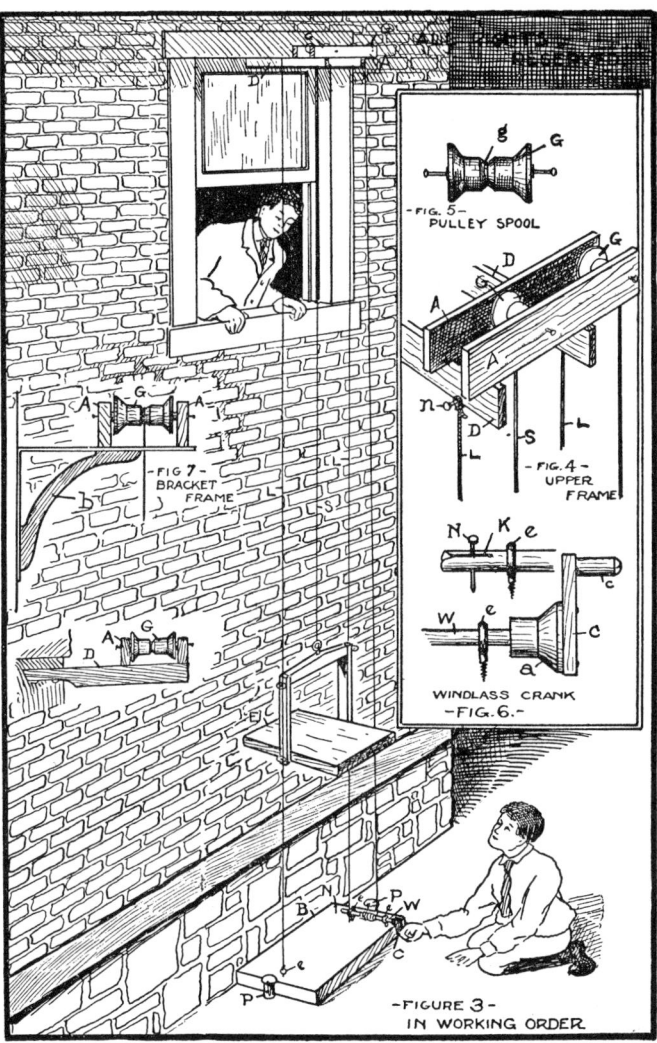

D. These are mounted in place by plugging up the central spool hole with a piece of wood that just fits, in its length, between the pieces *A*. Where the spools are to be mounted, bradawl holes are made through *A* on either side, and brads or needles driven through these holes, in which they should fit loosely into the ends of the spool plugs. This is shown in *Figures 5* and *7*, and you can see how mounting the spools in this way will make them turn very easily.

Mount your frame in the window top as shown in *Figure 3*, fasten a piece of board to the ground directly below with two screw eyes in it at *e* for your guide strings to fasten to, — the board is held down by the stakes *P*, — and we are ready to make the elevator car.

This may be made of a piece of flat board with a supporting frame over it, or you can use a cigar box *E*, as I have said, which will be better, for then things can't roll off.

Make the frame as in *Figure 8* of thin wood. Two side pieces run up for several inches from the centers of the sides and are connected crosswise at the top by a heavier stick *R*.

MODEL ELEVATORS

In the center of *R* on top is a screw eye *e* for the strings to fasten to. On each side are two screw eyes *e* that the guide strings will run through, as you see at *L*.

We are now ready to string the guide wires.

Drive stout brads *n* into the pieces *D* on the outside and between the pieces *A*, *Figure 4*, that is, just halfway between them. From these run

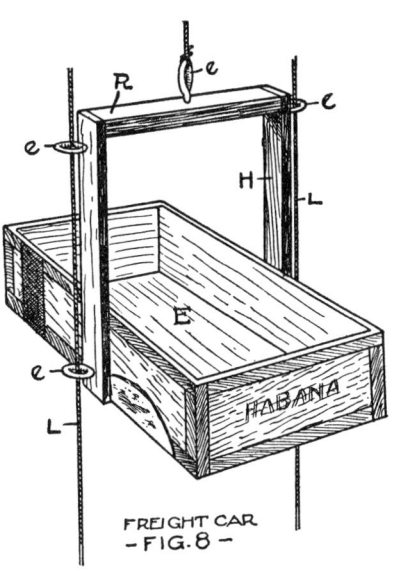

FREIGHT CAR
— FIG. 8 —

the strings down through the screw eyes *e* on the sides of the car and down to the screw eye in the baseboard on the ground at *P*. These strings should, of course, be tight, and you can see how they will keep the car from whirling or twisting when it is coming down.

Just to the right of where the right-hand

screw eye on the base *B* comes you will note a wooden shaft *W*, with a crank on one end, which the boy is turning. This is the hoisting windlass, which lifts the load, and it is shown in detail in *Figure 6*.

Here *W* is the stick which fits tightly into half a spool at *a*. You can make it doubly fast with glue.

The crank is made of a short stick with the piece *c* on its end, which is only a piece of spool with the flanges cut off and with a screw through the center hole. You may make it of just a nail, if you want to, driven into *C* at *c*.

The stick *W* fits through two screw eyes *e* as bearings, these being screwed into the base *B* at the proper places.

The other end of the stick *W* has a saw cut *K* in it, as in the upper *Figure 6*, and just opposite the end of the stick where it is mounted in the screw eyes is a brad *N* nailed into *B*.

Thus, when you want *W* to be held in any position, you can shove the shaft over till the nail is in the cut *K*, when the stick can't turn. When you want to turn it again, though, —

MODEL ELEVATORS

as when, for instance, you want to let the car down, — all you have to do is to pull the crank toward you till N is out of the cut K.

A string is now run from the screw eye on the crossbar of the elevator car, up around the spools, and down to the stick W, where it is wound around several times and fastened. When the elevator car is at the bottom, this string will be wound around a few times so it won't slip on W.

Now, when we turn the crank, W turns, and the string winds up, thus pulling the car E up. When we wish it to stop, then we stop turning the crank, and by slipping the stick W back until N is in the cut K, the car will be held at that position until we are ready to pull it up higher or let it down again.

If you want to make the frame at the top stronger, you can use common shelf brackets b, *Figure 7*, instead of the pieces D, fastening them in place with screws.

This elevator will furnish a lot of fun, and all that is required to make the car go up and down is the turning of a crank.

AN HYDRAULIC ELEVATOR

Another elevator just like this as to guide strings and general mechanism can be made to work by water power, so that you will not need to turn a crank or do anything but work levers to make the car go up and down as much as you want, so long as you keep the box at the top full of "fuel."

This "fuel" is ordinary water, which, by acting as a counterweight, makes the elevator run up and down along its guide wires.

Figure 9 shows this type of elevator in use at the back of a flat building, with two boys at work, while the third is looking on.

Figure 10 shows the mechanism of the elevator, while *Figures 11* and *12* show details on the counterbalance can.

The box at the top is an ordinary starch box of wood, painted inside to make it waterproof. From the small nails on the front face at *d* strings run down as guides to the elevator, as in the toy we made previously. Similar strings off to the other side from nails *b* take the guide strings for the counterweight can *C*.

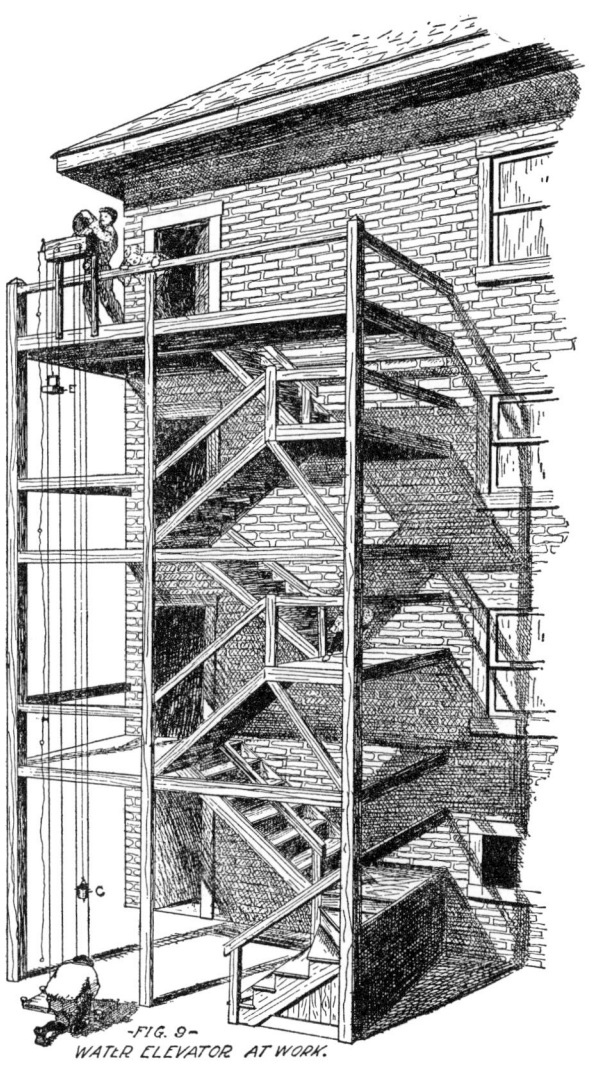

-FIG. 9-
WATER ELEVATOR AT WORK.

Two pulleys *J* made of sawed-off sections of curtain pole, with "V" grooves filed around the rim, are fastened to the front of the box halfway between the guide wires for the elevator and the can, so that the string *L*, passing around these pulleys, will run down centrally between the guide strings *d* and *b*. These pulleys should work loosely on the screws on which they pivot. A brake lever *B* is fixed over the pulley shown, so that when one pulls on the string which runs down from the outer end to the ring *R* at the bottom, a brake is set, and the elevator thus stopped at any floor. This brake lever is cut to fit the groove of the pulley *J* and has a rubber band *r* fitted between two nails shown, to hold the brake lever away from the pulley when not in use.

On the one end of the string *L* is fastened the elevator *E*, made as in the drawing of the former elevator, with a cigar box as the carrier.

On the other end of the string between the two guide strings or wires *b* is the tin can shown in *Figure 11*, which will need a little separate description.

In the bottom of this can is soldered a short

MODEL ELEVATORS

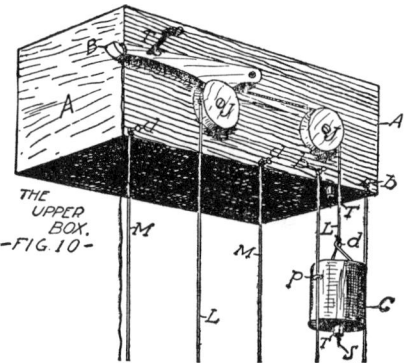

THE UPPER BOX.
—FIG. 10—

piece of tubing *T*, as shown in *Figure 12* in detail, this tubing being from the handle of an umbrella or bicycle pump and about half an inch long

FIG 10
THE LOWER PART.

After this is soldered in place, an ordinary

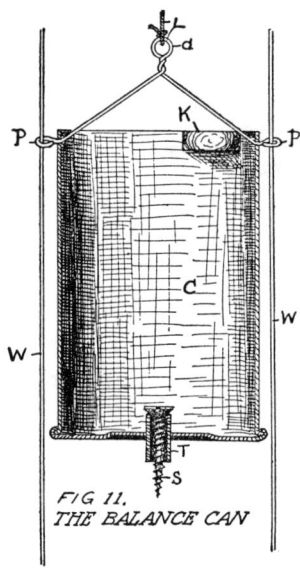

FIG 11.
THE BALANCE CAN

wood screw is taken with small notches *n* filed as its slanting face, as in the small sketch in *Figure 12*. Put this in the tube, as at *S* and rotate with a screwdriver while pressing down heavily on the screw. This will cut the edge of the tube at the same angle as the screw head, so that when a new screw *without the notches* is put into the tube, we have a water-tight valve. The weight of the screw will keep this tube from allowing any water to go through, but by lifting the screw from its seat, the water will run out of the can. At the top a loop *d* for the main string *L* is formed of a piece of wire, while the ends or arms from this run out through holes in the side of

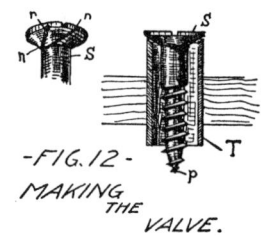

-FIG. 12-
MAKING THE VALVE.

MODEL ELEVATORS

the can near its upper edge and opposite each other, terminating in little loops p which act as guides for the strings W to run through, as shown. The string L is of such a length that when the elevator E is within half an inch, say, of the baseboard, the can is at the top, with its upper edge resting on the bottom of the box containing the water.

When in this position a hole which comes out into the top of this can, is bored through the bottom of the wooden box and into this hole is forced tightly another valve tube T with a valve screw S in it just like the one in the bottom of the can, while a small wooden block K is nailed to the inside of the can at its upper edge, so placed that when the can comes up to the top, this block K will hit the lower end of the screw valve in the bottom of the wooden box and open it. Supposing the box to be full of water, you can now see how the toy works.

The elevator is naturally heavier than the water can C, so that if left alone, the elevator drops to the ground, and the can goes up, the elevator being stopped wherever desired by

BOY'S BOOK OF MECHANICAL MODELS

the operator by pulling on the brake string previously described. As the elevator gets to the bottom, the can gets to the top, and the block K lifts the valve in the box, thus allowing the water to run out of the box into the tin can. This water will run until the can gets heavier than the elevator. The can will then start to descend, pulling up the elevator, and whatever load is in it. As the tin can descends, the elevator will be stopped at the different floors by means of the brake string.

As the elevator gets to the top, the can gets to the bottom; the screw S hits the trough or a stick arranged

MODEL ELEVATORS

at the bottom, and the valve T in the can is opened, thus allowing the water in the can to run onto the ground until the can becomes light enough so that the elevator starts down and the can starts up.

From this description you see that as long as you keep the box upstairs full of water, the elevator will keep traveling up and down, and can only be stopped by the use of the brakes for different floors. Be careful about the location of the tube in the box so that the block K will always hit it at the end of the up trip.

This elevator is not nearly so hard to make as it may sound at first, and the only job which may puzzle you is soldering the tube T into the bottom of the can C. If you punch the hole in the bottom of the can with the handle end of a file and have the tube all cut, any tinsmith will solder this for you for nothing, or for a few cents at least.

Figure 9 shows this toy working up four flights, but if desired it can be run to almost unlimited height so long as the weight of the string on the one side does not overbalance the weight of the can of water, or the difference in weight between the elevator and the can. If you do not want to use water, by a little ingenuity you can work with sand as power.

No toy elevator ever devised will give you more fun than this one.

A Perpetual Calendar

HERE is a new kind of calendar that will last for years, so far as correct showing of dates is concerned, while to change it to the new date every day it is only necessary to pull down a small lever.

FIG. 1.

This shows the number on the dial *A* through a little square hole *H* in the back of the cigar-box case, in which the calendar is set, as shown at the right of *Figure 1*.

Every thirty-one pulls of the lever — that is, at the end of every thirty days — the next dial B is moved when the control is pulled, so as to show up a new month in the slot b.

If there are only thirty days in the month, then pull the lever twice on the "30th" and the dial will show number 1 and change the month reading.

If desired, the lever can be worked by a string running down to a wire ring O, which can be pulled every day to change the date.

Make the works carefully and this calendar will last for years. The mechanism is not hard to understand, and the only thing that requires special care is the marking out of the parts.

One of these calendars has been in use for over a year with good success, and it was made from the crude material described in this article. The only repairs in all that time were replacing the rubber band, which got old and had to be renewed every few months.

The big dial A was made of half-inch wood, about four inches in diameter, and was cut as true as possible with a knife. Around its rim even spaces were marked off. There were

A PERPETUAL CALENDAR

thirty-one of them, and at each space a cut was sawed, just a quarter of an inch deep, to meet a circle drawn a quarter of an inch in-

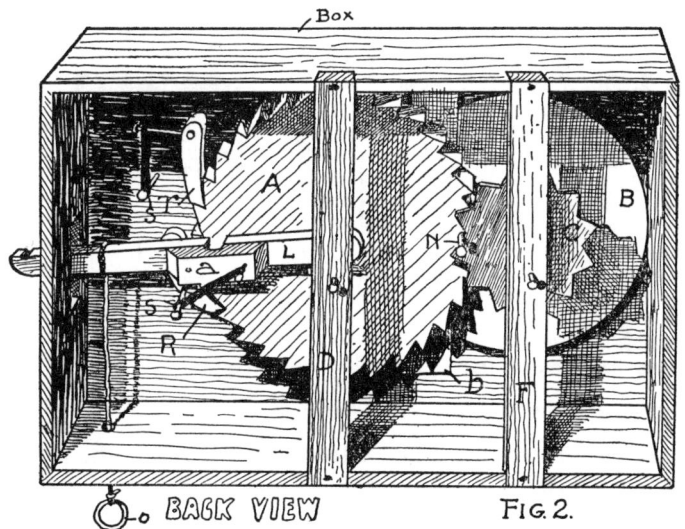

Fig. 2.

side the rim of this wheel *A*. Then with a knife the parts next to these cuts were slanted off to resemble a lot of teeth, all facing one way as shown.

This wheel was fitted tightly to a quarter-inch shaft and was placed in the box temporarily between needle bearings *n, n* in the box bottom on one end and a cross stick *D, Figures* **2** and *3*, at the other. The location of this wheel *A* is shown in the same figures.

On the shaft of this wheel was loosely pivoted a lever *L*. This lever was made of

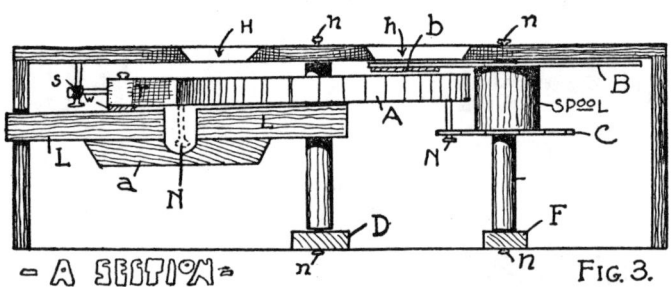

FIG. 3.

two pieces connected by a "bridge" piece *a*, leaving a gap through which a nail *N* on the rim of *A* could pass when *A* turned, without hitting the lever *L*. The gap is easily seen in *Figure 3* with the nail (dotted) going through.

Back of the wheel on the box bottom was fastened a little "pawl," as it is called, as at *r*, *Figure 5*, with a rubber band *s* stretched between small nails, as shown at *e* and *f*, to serve as a spring to hold the pawl against the notches of *A*. This lets the wheel *A* turn in one direction, but will not allow it to turn back.

A PERPETUAL CALENDAR

On the lever was another pawl *R*, *Figure 4*, with a rubber band spring somewhat similar. This also pressed against *A*. The lever *L*

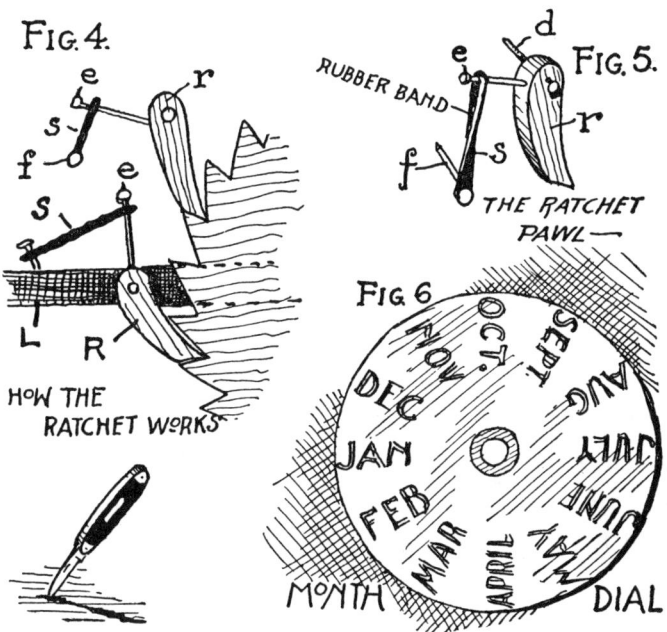

itself stuck out through the end of the box through a slot, as shown in *Figure 2*, the length of the slot determining how far the lever could be pulled each time. This length was so made that every pull would let the pawl *R* slide over one notch as the lever went up — a rubber

161

band pulling it — while the upper pawl r kept the wheel A from moving back with it.

Pulling down, the first pawl R stuck to A and the second pawl r slipped, so that the wheel was turned the length of one notch, as you can plainly see.

On the other side of the box bottom a square hole H was cut through near the rim of the wheel A. On the back of A and on a paper glued to it the numbers 1 to 31 were written, showing through the box hole H as the wheel was turned a notch at a time by the lever L.

This done, the wheel was removed from the box, and the "month" dial made. This was a thin pasteboard dial B tacked to a piece of spool as shown in *Figure 3*. At the other end of the spool was a tin circle C with twelve star-points all spaced equally and equally deep. This was fastened to the spool end with small brads. Care was taken to get it centrally located.

The dial was slipped under the wheel A on one side, as shown, with the spool just clearing the saw-edge of A. The wooden shaft running through the spool was pivoted between the

A PERPETUAL CALENDAR

box bottom and the cross stick F by needles n, n.

A paper piece b was glued to the box bottom and stretched over B, where it came under A, so A in turning would not rub against B and move it before its time. The small nail N was next fitted into a hole made carefully in A at the rim, back of the number 1, so that when N came by, it would turn B one star point at a time. The nail N was inserted carefully into a tight hole so as not to split a tooth off A.

After the parts were all fitted right, the whole thing was put together. B was mounted first and made to turn snugly — not too easily. Then A was fixed in place, the lever L fastened on with its ratchet pawl R, and finally the cross stick outside at D.

Now, on pulling the string tied to the lever L and which ran down through a hole in the box, the wheel A turned as before, but at every revolution, when N came past the star C, this was turned one tooth by the nail N. The nail was put in at the number 1 on A, so that the shift of C came at the first of the month.

All that then remained was to mark the months on B through the hole h on the other side, as the twelve positions came into view by working the lever string.

A coat of varnish added to the box was the only thing needed to complete the job. A calendar of this kind is a real novelty.

A Threshing Machine

I REMEMBER one autumn spent on a farm during threshing time and what fun we boys had riding loads and making our own threshing machine.

Perhaps some of my readers would like to make one too, so here it is shown in these drawings and you can put through it what you want — oats, or breakfast food, or dried grass. But whatever you throw in at the table G on one end will be thrown out and stacked at the other. When you want to move to a new locality, you can raise the stacker by turning the crank K, thus closing up the table G and the floor or platform P at the other end and off you go. You can pick up the things to make the thresher from around the house.

First you take a cigar box and cut out the front lower end as shown in *Figure 1*. Then you knock both ends out, being careful not to split the wood.

Along the bottom sides run two strips *C* of quarter-inch wood from some old box and connect them up front by a cross bar.

At the back they stick out a little, so the platform *P*, of thin wood from a cigar box or

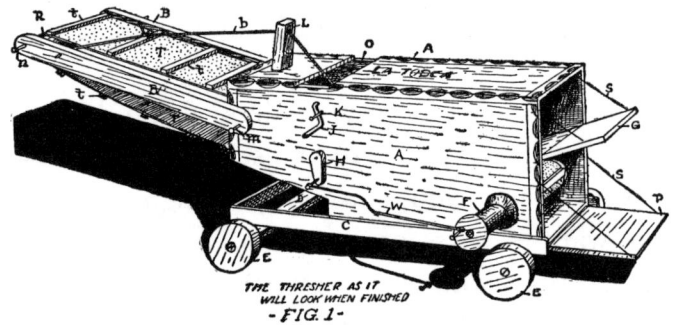

THE THRESHER AS IT WILL LOOK WHEN FINISHED
- *FIG. 1* -

other wood, can be pivoted on them to fold up against the end when you are ready to move.

In front two strips *B*, *Figure 1*, run out from the sides of the box and are connected a couple of inches from their outer end by a cross bar, as in *Figure 3* at *d*, where the frame of the stacker is shown. At the extreme end of these pieces a spool *R*, with the enlarged ends trimmed down even, or a piece of broomstick, is pivoted between two brads *n*, through loose holes in *B* so it can turn.

A THRESHING MACHINE

Inside the box and toward the rear a second roller made of a spool, as in the drawing of the spool drive, *Figure 3*, is fixed on a shaft which sticks through a hole in one side of the

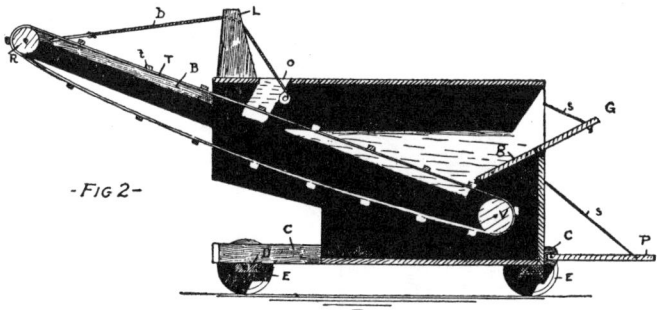

THRESHER WITH SIDE OFF SHOWING MACHINERY

box, so a spool pulley F can fit on tightly. The other end is pivoted through the opposite side of the box by a brad n. Little disks r of cardboard or tin can be put on both rollers if the belt tends to run off, but this won't bother if you are careful to get the roller in the box exactly parallel with the one R at the end of the pieces B.

The belt is of canvas or cloth or of wide tape and has little strips of wood t sewed or glued across it every inch or less to carry the load. It is run over the two pulleys as shown

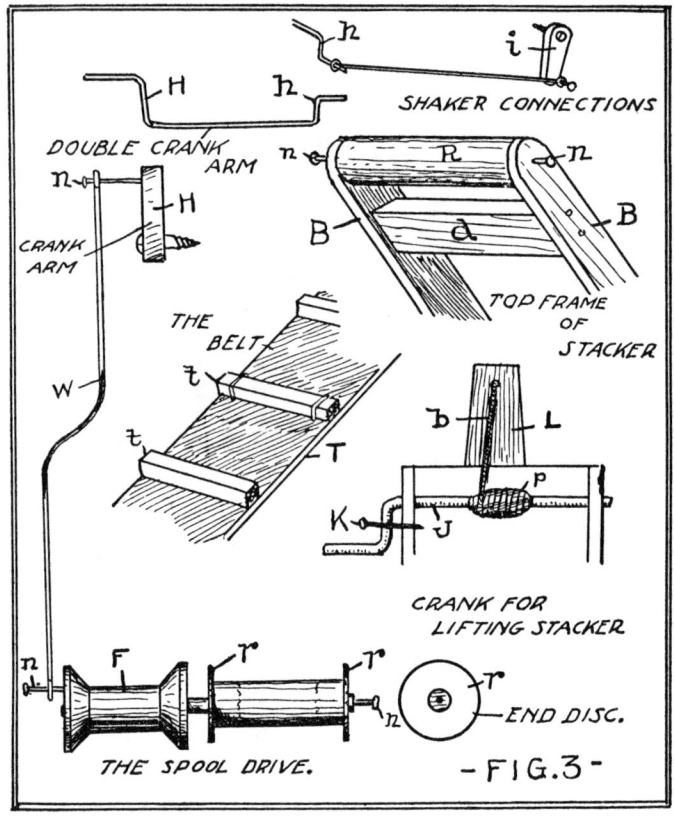

in *Figure 2* and is turned by a crank fastened to spool pulley F.

If you want a shaker on the side, you can run a wire W from a brad on the spool end F to a little crank H fastened to the box side

A THRESHING MACHINE

with a brad, as shown in *Figures 1* and *3*, or you can make a wire crank here and run it clear through the box and have the wooden crank arrangement on the other side of the box from a crank *h* on the wire *H* on that side, *Figure 3*. This crank arm, of course, has to be bent after it is inserted in the sides *A*.

Before putting the stacker on, fix up the post *L*, and the wire crank *J*, running through the sides of the box so it will wind up the string *b* and, pulling through the hole in *L*, lift the stacker as shown in *Figure 1* and *3*. A nail *K*, fitting loosely into a hole in the side of the box next to the crank can be stuck in when you want to hold the stacker in any set position.

It is easy to see how the doors at the rear are fixed to turn up and are held at the proper place when down by the threads or strings *s*. Inside the box fix a piece of wood at *g* running down just far enough to clear the belt, to guide the material down from the platform *G*.

The wheels can be made of pieces of curtain pole or checker men and fastened on any way you like.

A Walking Horse

ALL kinds of things can be made from cigar boxes, but the toy described next is one I used to make for some of the smaller boys about birthday time, and it always gave them a great deal of amusement. It is better shown in the drawing, *Figure 1*.

This is a "walking" horse, whose body is nothing but a cigar box, so arranged, with pivoted wooden legs and a string to work it by, that when you pull on this string or thread back of the toy, it will walk away from you. It is very easy to see how this toy works.

In the first place, the head and tail are cut from cigar-box wood and are fastened in place by small nails or even pins. The front legs are cut out of cigar-box wood and are fastened rigidly to the body of the toy by small nails, so that there is no pivoting.

The hind legs are pivoted on a wire P at the lower corner of the box, while about half

A WALKING HORSE

an inch above a cross wire C connects these two pieces, running through slots H instead of holes, so that the hind legs are free to move

Fig. 1.

backward and forward on the lower wire as a pivot.

A spacer of wire having a loop in the middle connects the front legs near the bottom. The hind legs are connected in the same way, the wire running through holes in the wood near the feet.

A rubber band inside the body of the toy, shown at R, pulls forward on the upper cross wire of the hind legs, so that normally this rubber band keeps them pushing backward as far as the lever action of these side pieces is allowed by the slot *H*, *Figure 2*.

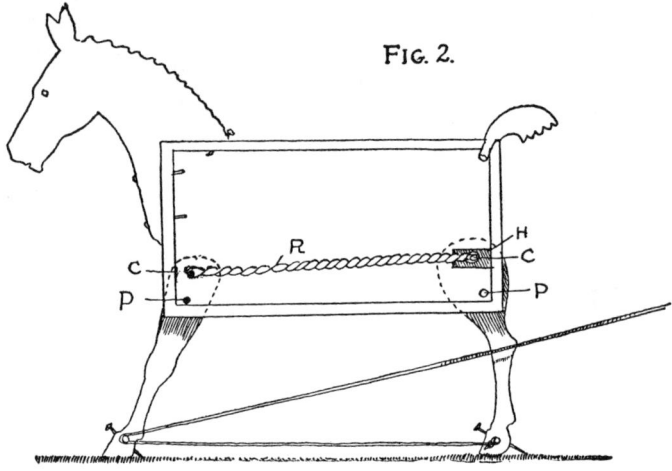

FIG. 2.

A string or thread runs through the loop in the lower foot wire of the hind leg pieces, runs forward through the loop in the front wire, and back, as shown in *Figure 1*.

You can very easily see that when this string is pulled, it will move the hind legs forward, thus stretching the rubber band *R*, and that when the string is released, the rubber band *R* will pull them back again.

A WALKING HORSE

Through the feet of the horse are driven pins at an angle as shown in *Figure 2*, pointing backward and projecting about one-eighth of an inch. These are slanted at an angle of forty-five degrees at least, so that they may slide forward, but will not slide backward without sticking into the carpet.

Set this toy on the floor, and pull on the thread or operating string. The hind feet are drawn forward toward the front feet, since the pins in the front feet hold the toy from sliding backward on the carpet, while the pins in the rear feet slide forward over the nap of the carpet without difficulty. On releasing the string, the rubber band R immediately tends to push the rear feet back. This forces the pins in the hind feet into the carpet and causes them to thrust the whole toy forward. The front feet then slide forward, the pins in the front feet being automatically withdrawn from the carpet to allow the toy to move. Thus the alternate pulling and releasing of the string causes the feet to come together and push apart.

You can make this toy with nothing but a jacknife, some nails, and a hairpin, if you have to, — I mean with a very small equipment, — but if you have some shop tools, it will help, of course, in cutting out your patterns.

FIG. 3.

In *Figure 3* are shown the patterns for the head and tail pieces of the toy. *Figure 4* shows patterns for the legs. You can enlarge these to any size to fit the cigar box which you are going to use.

You would do well to lay the cigar box on its side first on a piece of paper and mark around it so as to get a rectangle just its size. On this paper sketch out the head and tail and legs in proportion to the size of your cigar-box body.

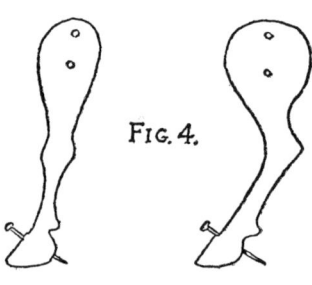
FIG. 4.

When the final pattern is made on paper, cut out the shapes and paste them on cigar-box wood. Then with a fret saw or even your knife cut around the pattern carefully.

A WALKING HORSE

The front legs can be fastened to the cigar-box body with small nails, although in the drawing I have shown cross wires, since, as I said before, the front legs are fastened rigidly to the box.

Make the pivot point on the hind legs three quarters of an inch or an inch below the top of the pattern. Through the holes punched at this point fit hairpin wire as a pivot running through small holes in the cigar box near the lower corner as at *P*. These holes in the cigar box should not be too loose, but should be large enough so that the wire can turn freely without binding.

Bore a hole in the hind legs half an inch above this pivoting wire and connect through the body of the toy by another wire having a loop in its center, as do the wires which are attached at the feet of the toy. This wire does not run through a mere hole in the body, but through a slot *H* which allows it to move back and forth for a short space, say about three-eighths of an inch. Stretch a rubber band from the loop in the center of this wire to the cross wire between the front legs, or to a nail in the other end of the box.

This rubber band must be strong enough to push the toy across the carpet and yet should not be too strong, or the pull required on the string to stretch it will be too great. You will need to experiment with the tension of this rubber band.

The cross wires at the feet are made of hairpin wire bent as shown and fitting tightly through holes in the foot pieces. If these are too loose, the wire may be wrapped around the ankle of the pattern to hold it tight.

The drawings show how the operating string runs forward through the loop in the wire connecting the front feet, so that when you pull on the string, the front bar merely acts as a pulley to draw the front and hind feet together.

When the hind feet have moved as far as the length of the slots H allows, release the string, and the rubber band R will push the feet back again and thus thrust the toy forward by catching the pins in the carpet. This toy will not work on a smooth floor.

A Walking Policeman

THE body part of this policeman is cut of thin cigar-box wood after the pattern of *Figures 1* and *2*, which can be traced off or enlarged by squares to fit the piece of wood you have. Do not try to make the body less than six inches high.

Figure 2 shows the machinery that makes the man walk. The pattern for the legs is clearly outlined. This is cut from half-inch wood and proportioned to the size of the body.

The driving wheel is shown at *W*. Make a circle on a piece of cigar-box wood large enough to just fit in the position shown and not project beyond the sides. Make another circle a quarter or three-eighths of an inch inside of this, and then divide the outer one into twelve parts.

Do the same with the inner one, seeing that the divisions come just halfway between those on

Fig. 1

READY TO START OFF

the outer circle, and then connect the dots with lines. This will mark out a twelve-pointed star wheel, as you see at *W*. This wheel has a hole *n* bored in its center, and is then mounted

A WALKING POLICEMAN

FIG. 2.

on a small half-spool *E*, *Figure 3*, as a hub. Another spool is now tightly mounted on a shaft *D* of wood as at *S*. This spool has six notches cut in one rim, as in the drawing of the ratchet in *Figure 5*, the notches being at *J*.

BOY'S BOOK OF MECHANICAL MODELS

The wooden spool shaft sticks out of one end of this spool far enough to run through the wheel *W* and its spool hub *E*, which turn loosely on it. The hub *S*, as I said before, is tight on the shaft *D*.

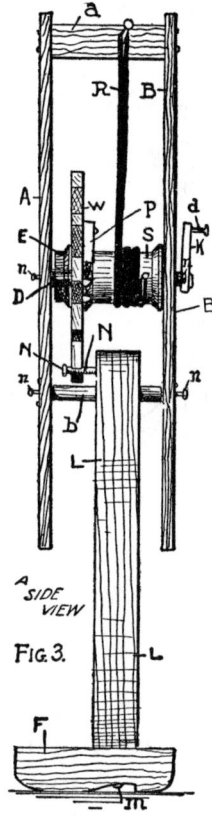

SIDE VIEW
FIG. 3.

Now in the back piece *B* bore a hole through which this shaft *D* will fit loosely, and opposite it, in *A*, bore a small hole for the brad *n* to fit loosely through.

Stick the back end of the shaft *D* through the hole in *B* and square off what projects through, so that you can fix a crank *K* on it. On *W* itself fix a little wooden "pawl" *P*, in the ratchet drawing, *Figure 5*, with a rubber band *r* to pull it against the rim of the spool, so that when the spool turns one way the pawl *P* will slip over the notches, and will catch when the spool turns the other way. Now, through the piece

180

A WALKING POLICEMAN

you have cut out for the legs, bore a small hole at *b*, *Figure 2*, and mount through it a shaft *b*, *Figure 3*, the same length as shaft *D* above, on which the spool *S* is mounted.

Make a hole in *B* directly under the hole through which *D* runs and just far enough below so that when the wheel *W* turns it will not hit shaft *b*, which is mounted in this hole by a brad driven into the end of the shaft, as at *n*. A similar hole is made in *A*, just opposite, for the other end of this shaft, which is fastened there with another brad *n*.

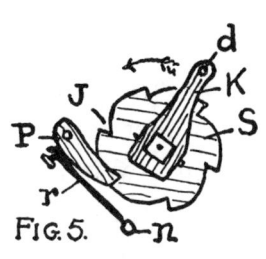

Next cut three sticks about a sixteenth of an inch longer than the shafts *D* and *b*, and fasten the pieces *A* and *B* together temporarily, nailing the piece *a* across at the head and the pieces *C* at either side of the hips. The pieces *C* are not shown in the side view, but their location is indicated in *Figure 2* and you can see *a* at the top of *Figure 3*.

If everything fits well, take *A* off again, and into *L* drive two shingle nails *N*, whose distance apart is such that when *W* turns, one nail *N* is on top of a star point of W when the other is clear at the bottom of the *V*, as in *Figure 4*.

Now, if you put *A* on again and hold *A–B* in your hand, — that is, the body part of the policeman, — the legs will swing like a pendulum when you turn *W*, for the points of the star will push the nails *N* out and in as the wheel *W* turns.

But we cannot stand and turn *W* ourselves, so we must fix a spring, and the most common kind is one of rubber bands. Drive a small tack into *S*, *Figure 3*, and hook one end of the rubbers *R* to it. Then run them round *S* in the same direction that the ratchet catches and up to a nail on *a* at the head. Wind the toy up by turning the crank *K* on the end of the shaft *D*. Though the spool *S* turns, and the rubber winds up, *W* does not turn, for the pawl slips over the notches in the spool rim *S*. When we release the crank, though, the rubber band pulls the spool around, the pawl catches,

A WALKING POLICEMAN

and the wheel W turns, thus wobbling the legs. Make the feet of blocks F, as shown, and nail them on at the bottom of the legs as at m, *Figure 3*.

Nail A on. Drive the brads that pivot D and b at the front into their positions through the holes you have made for them, and be sure that W can turn all the way around without catching. It will not catch if you have marked and cut the wheel W carefully. The shaft b should be as near to the rim of W as possible without hitting, and the nails N should be equally distant from b and as far apart, as I said before, as the distance from the top of one star tooth to the bottom of the second distant from it, as in *Figure 4*.

Now set the policeman on an incline and wind up the crank. When you let him go, his legs will swing and his body will move.

The Pendulum of Galileo

AWAY back in the year 1564 a boy was born in Pisa, Italy, who could do almost anything he started out to do. He had gifts, it seemed, in all directions, and he could practically choose in which line he wished to be great.

In the first place he was a fine musician and wrote a book on the theory and practice of music. He was very skilled as a player of the lute, — one of the musical instruments common in those days, — and it was as a player that we first hear of his genius.

Finally this boy, who came of a fine family, was put to school and showed that he was a brilliant scholar. His father wanted him to be a doctor, so finally he studied medicine and would have made a famous doctor if something else hadn't interested him.

In 1583, while he was standing in the cathedral at Pisa, — you have doubtless read the story in school, — he saw a bronze lamp which

THE PENDULUM OF GALILEO

was suspended from the ceiling by a chain swinging back and forth, and he soon noticed that each swing took the same amount of time, whether the lamp swung through a wide arc or a small one. He immediately applied the idea to a small machine, — somewhat in the nature of a clock, — made to measure pulse beats. He had no knowledge of arithmetic or mathematics, or he might have gone farther with this invention at this time.

But suddenly he lost his interest in medicine and took up mathematics. One day he overheard one Ostilio Ricci, a teacher, giving lessons in mathematics to some of the pages in the court of the duke then living at Pisa. Immediately the youth became intensely interested and studied so hard that a short time later, when Ricci went on to another town, he took this boy Galileo with him to show off his knowledge.

Next we hear of him as the famous inventor of a piece of scientific apparatus, — the "hydrostatic balance." And so he went on, writing and inventing and growing more famous every day. He didn't use much tact, though, so he

BOY'S BOOK OF MECHANICAL MODELS

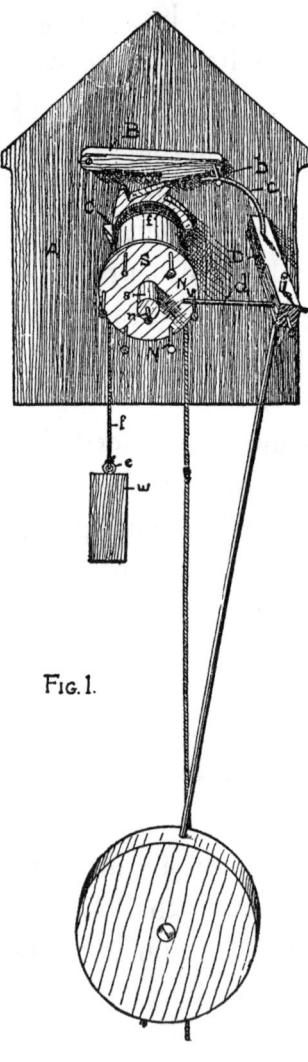

Fig. 1.

made some enemies, and that was a dangerous thing in those days.

For instance, the professors of a certain college said, all of them, that a body fell with a speed according to its size; that is, a cannon ball would fall twice as fast as one half as large. When they all said it, — and it was considered a law of science in those days, — Galileo took them out on the leaning tower of Pisa and by actual experiment proved they were wrong. Of course they didn't like this, and as a result the young man lost his job.

THE PENDULUM OF GALILEO

Then he invented the thermometer and some say the telescope also. At least, he was the first to really use one in astronomy.

I saw a model of his pendulum in the South Kensington Museum in London, and his own drawing that it was made from was there too. When I got home I made a little model of it, and it worked perfectly and ticked away as merrily as a real clock. *Figure 1* shows the pendulum.

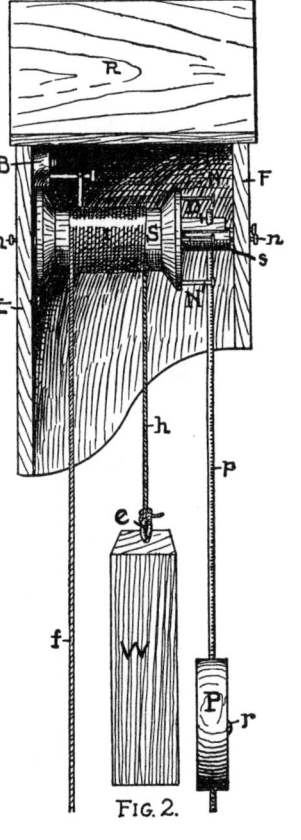

FIG. 2.

First the spool S is fixed to turn by a weight below. Six nails N are driven in one end of the spool at equal distances around the edge, while on the other end of the spool the flange, or edge, is cut with six notches opposite the nails.

Over it is the pawl B that drops down into the notches and keeps the spool from turning. There is a piece D at the side with the pendulum hanging from it. From this piece D a wire c runs out so it can swing up and hit the nail b that sticks out from B and lift B up out of the notch. Then the spool can turn.

Another wire d runs out from the stick D under one of the nails on the end of the spool, *Figure 1*. When the spool S starts to turn, the nail N pushes down on this wire d, and this swings the pendulum to the right. This movement lets the wire c down, and the pawl B catches the next notch on the spool and holds it so it cannot turn any more till the pendulum swings back again. When it swings back the wire c will lift B again. So long as the weight turns the spool, the pendulum will swing back and forth, once for every notch, six times for every turn of the spool.

Now about making the model.

The spool S is mounted on a tight wooden axle s with needles or brads on the ends to turn on, as at n. The brads N are nailed in place, as you see in *Figure 1*, and the axle s

THE PENDULUM OF GALILEO

sticks out enough so that when the spool is mounted in a frame, as in *Figure 2*, the nails have plenty of room without hitting the frame.

The frame can be made as in the separate drawings, *Figures 3* and *4*, — *3* being the pattern for the ends, which are cut of thin cigar-box wood with a keyhole saw, and *4* giving a picture of the finished frame from the front.

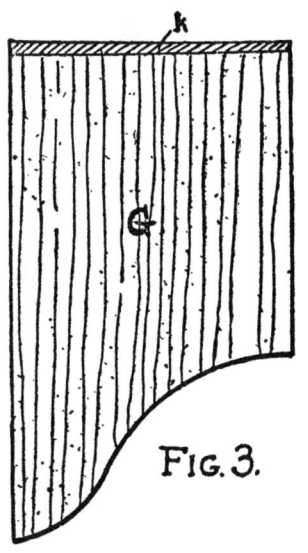

FIG. 3.

Of course, you needn't make the frame just like this. For instance, instead of the wooden axle *s*, you could use a large screw and hold up the outer end of *D* by a wire bracket. Then all your machinery would be in sight. If you want to inclose it, this form shown by *Figures 3* and *4* is good, and you can fasten a hand to the outer end of *n* to turn like the second hand of a watch, — only faster.

If you like, instead of a spool, you could

cut a larger wheel with little pegs in the rim and with sixty little brads in the face. Then you could lengthen the pendulum to beat once

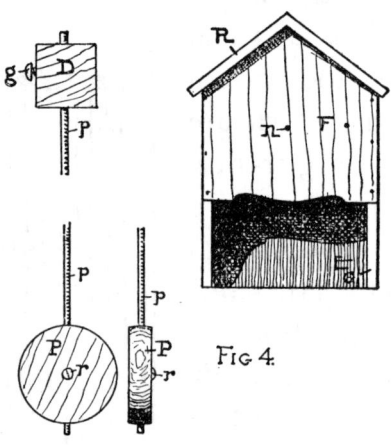

Fig 4.

a second, and your wheel would turn once a minute (60 seconds), just like the second hand of a watch.

The pawl piece *B*, *Figure 1*, is cut from a piece of half-inch wood and pivoted on a brad or a small screw. The nail *b* at its other end may be a shingle nail.

The piece *D* needs to be only half an inch square, and you can see in the small sketch of *Figure 4* how the wires are fastened to it

THE PENDULUM OF GALILEO

with a small screw *g*. The holes may be bored so the wires will be a tight fit.

Figure 4 will show also how to hang the pendulum. This is just a round piece of wood *P*, weighted with lead, perhaps, that is fitted on a wire *p*. By sliding the wood up and down on the wire, you can vary the time the pendulum will swing.

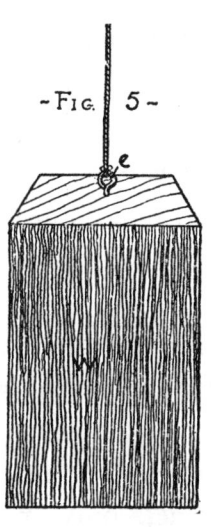

-Fig. 5-

The weights are to keep the string on the spool tight and to wind the machine up. The big one does the work, and when it goes down, — the string is wound several times around the spool *S*, — the little weight goes up. When it gets clear up, you can hold the pendulum off to one side so the nails *N* won't hit the wire *d* and pull the little weight down. This will lift the big weight again, and the "clock" will be "wound up."

These weights can be made of a piece of wood squared, with a screw eye *c* in the top; or you can bore a hole in the bottom of them and pour in lead, if you want them heavier.

A Siren Whistle

DID you ever hear a siren whistle, — the kind that goes from a low note to a high note and then down again as it blows? Would you like to make one?

First take a paper roll — or maybe you haven't any. Well, then, roll some paper around a stick, a round stick, say a little over a quarter of an inch through or even half an inch. I made one once with a piece of broomstick to wind the paper around, and it worked fine, only my bellows wasn't quite strong enough to blow it well.

Put paste or glue on the paper and wind it around the stick, being careful that the stick doesn't get glued on, and hold the piece in a vise, or in some such way that it won't slip until it is dry. You can see how this is done in the drawings, *Figure 1*.

After it is all dry, cut the notch *n* in the tube about an inch from one end. This is

A SIREN WHISTLE

shown in my drawing of "Cutting the tube," *Figure 1.*

Take out the stick and cut a piece from it an inch long as at *a*, the "wind block," and along one side cut off a thin slice, as at *m*.

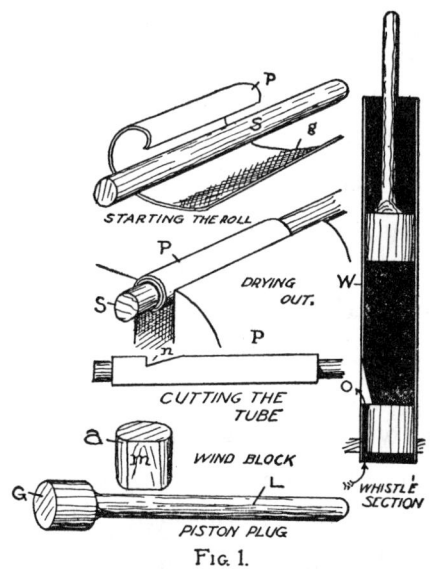

Fig. 1.

Thus when you put the block back in the end of the tube, there will be a space *O* left between the tube and the block so that the wind can come up through it and out of the notch *n* that we cut. This wind block is shown at the bottom of the tube in the drawing "whistle section." It is shown at *a* in *Figure 5*. The tube we have made of paper is shown at *W*, *Figure 1*.

Now take the rest of the stick *S* and from it form a plunger *G*, or piston plug which will fit into the top part of the tube *W* and slide up and down. Since the paper was rolled around it, the plug will be a good fit and nearly air-tight.

Now put the whistle in your mouth and blow. If it does not whistle, the opening *O* cut from the wind block *a* is probably too small. Take the block out and cut off a larger slice. When it is all right, glue it firmly in place.

As the whistle blows, pull the piston plug in and out, and the note will vary like a true siren; with practice one can play a tune — whether it be music or not.

Then in a cigar-box cover at *E*, *Figure 2*, bore a half-inch hole. Under the hole glue a piece of thin leather *V*, with a piece of cardboard *e* fastened below to act as a stiffener or spring. These are glued along only one edge of the cover, so that the suction of the air can

A SIREN WHISTLE

pull the leather down and let the air in, as in the sketch of the valve open, *Figure 2*, and then, when the air tries to go the other way,

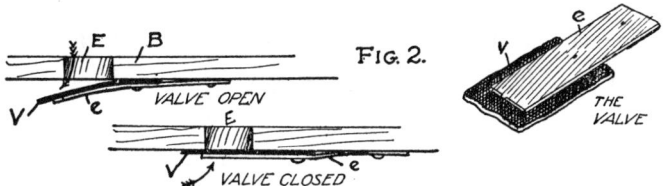

Fig. 2.

it will flop the leather up against the hole *E* again and close it. You see it must be fixed so that the air can go through one way and can't come back. Next fasten the cover down on the cigar box and paste up all the cracks with paper.

Then take a piece of half-inch board *B*, *Figures 4* and *5*, and cut it the shape of the box top, only an inch and a half shorter, and fix a similar valve in it the same way, *Figure 5* — to let the air in but not out. Before you fasten this valve on, though, you must make the bellows' sides.

Take a piece of stiff Manila wrapping paper and fold it, as at *A* in the series on "folding the bellows," *Figure 3*. The folds should not be over three quarters of an inch wide, and the strip should be say three times as long as the side of the box that we are using for the wind chest.

Next, as at *B*, fold the paper at right angles so as to fit around the edges of the board *B*

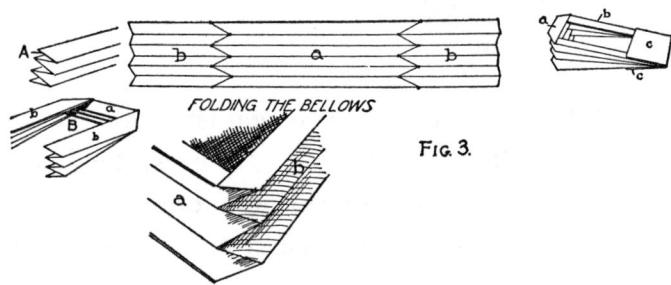

FOLDING THE BELLOWS

Fig. 3.

that makes the top of the bellows. Just fold it straight over and crease it hard.

When you straighten the strip out, you will find that the creases look like the parts *a*, *b*. Crease the folds *b* all the opposite way from what they now are, and the zigzag lines, too, down between *a* and the sides *b*; you will find that your corners are correctly turned, and will look as in the lower drawing of this series.

Lay this piece on the board *B* and cut off the ends so that the paper fits properly inside.

A SIREN WHISTLE

Over the sharp end of the wedge paste the Manila paper piece *c* as in the drawing at the extreme right.

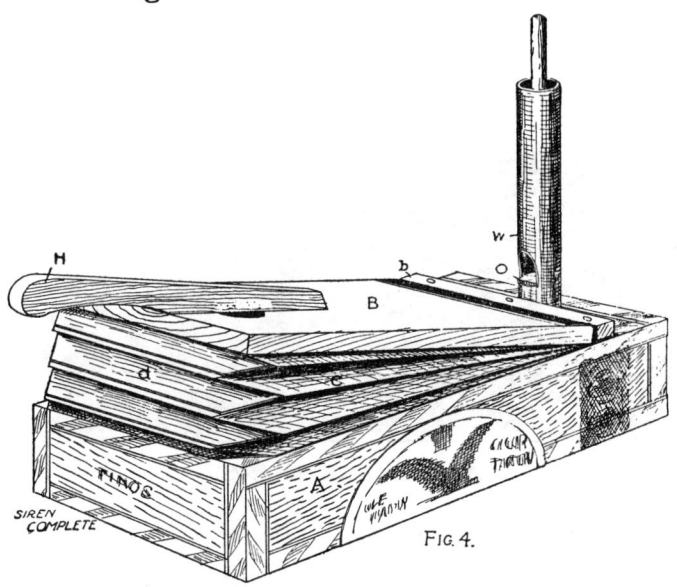

Fig. 4.

This makes the end air-tight. Paste the lower edges to the top of the box, and be careful to leave no gaps. Use liquid or fresh glue if you have it.

Smear glue on the upper flaps too, — that is, the upper edge of the paper bellows, — and press the board *B* down into position, holding it with a weight till dry. Be careful not to glue anything but just the upper strip. Watch the corners too and glue all openings there.

At the right hand of *B*, in *Figures 4* and *5*, you see a black strip. This is a strip of leather

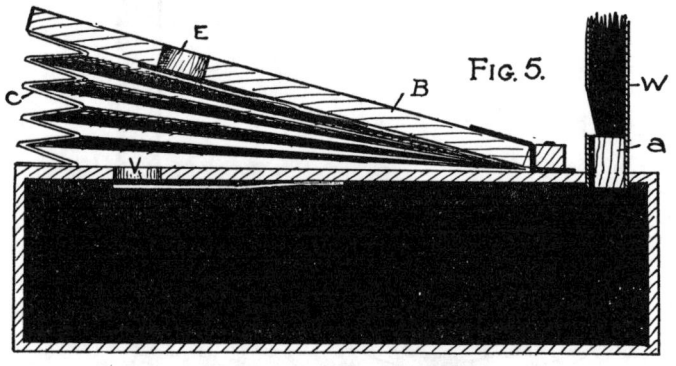

SECTION SHOWING VALVES.

running down under a wooden piece *b*, and which is glued to hold the lower edge of *B* secure, so it won't tear the paper.

Put on the handle *H*, bore a hole in the box, as in *Figure 5*, glue in the whistle you have made, and the siren is ready.

When you lift *H*, — thus lifting *B*, — the air is sucked in through the valve in *B*, which opens. Then push down on *B*, and the air closes the valve in *B* but opens the one *V* in

A SIREN WHISTLE

the cover of the box A, so that the wind rushes into the box and out through the whistle, with the expected result — a noise. So, by working the handle H up and down, the whistle blows.

If the bellows end tends to bulge out, paste paper or cardboard stiffeners at d, as shown.

A German "Thur-Zither"

SEVERAL summers ago I stopped for a few days at the home of an American dentist in Germany.

My host was a pleasant and entertaining gentleman, and his home was full of knickknacks and curios picked up in various parts of the continent, which he always enjoyed exhibiting.

On the first day of my visit, on entering the living room from the main hall, I noticed a faint yet beautiful strain of music, whose source puzzled me. It seemed to come from far off, faint at best, but easier to be heard from the side of the room toward the hall — yet I had heard no music when coming through the hall on the way to the living room.

The music was made by strings, as one could tell from the tone, and after a moment's listening I could see that there were only five notes in all, striking irregularly and making a beautiful minor chord, loud and soft, soft and loud, —

A GERMAN "THUR-ZITHER"

ghost music, intangible but sweet, — like the strains of an Æolian harp in a soft wind.

My host was still standing by the door as I stopped, turned, and listened, and his body hid what I should have seen. With his back to the door and his hands behind him, he was swinging it from time to time a few inches each way. As I looked up at him finally, with a puzzled expression, he burst out laughing.

"What is it?" I asked. "Where does it come from?"

For answer he stepped aside, and there on the back of the door was the machine shown in the drawings, — a thur-zither (pronounced "toor-zitter"), as he explained afterwards.

It was composed of a little box part, or sounding-board below, over which were stretched five steel strings. Supported a little above the box was a rod from which little lead balls were suspended on threads, a ball opposite each string, so that when the door was opened, the ball at the ends of the threads would tap against the strings.

With my host's consent, I made a sketch of the zither on the spot, and will tell you how to make one.

First, cut a piece of thin, straight-grained wood planed on both sides and a little less than a quarter of an inch thick. This, — the front piece of the zither, — is shown in the separate pattern drawing *Figure 1,* and at *A* in the picture, *Figure 4.*

Enlarge this pattern on paper and lay it on the piece of board (the grain running up and down); at the right of a center line drawn up its middle, trace the pattern. Then turn the pattern over, sliding it also over to the other side of the center line, and trace the other half of the zither front, which will then surely be the same on both sides.

Cut this piece out with a keyhole, or fret saw. One with a wire frame for small blades can be purchased at a hardware store for

FIG. 2.

A THUR-ZITHER

something like fifteen cents. The blades cost ten cents a dozen.

If you can't get a saw, it isn't a very hard job to cut the thin wood with a knife, if you are careful and keep your blade sharp.

The hole *e* in the center should be marked with a compass before cutting in order to get it as true as possible.

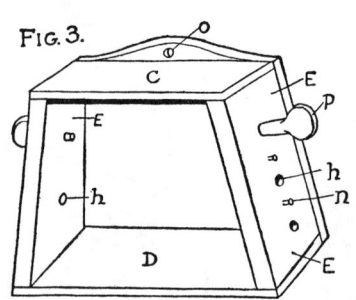

The back piece in the sketch of the sound box, *Figure 3*, is cut of the same kind of wood and is the same shape as the front, except that there is no top part above the dot-and-dash line *d* in the pattern *Figure 1*, and no hole in the center at *e*. The grain runs crosswise.

These two pieces are separated by a box part shown at the "sound box," *Figure 3*.

This consists of two end pieces *E* of wood a quarter or three-eighths of an inch thick, connected at top and bottom by strips *C* and *D*. Make this part as carefully as possible so that

A GERMAN "THUR-ZITHER"

the front and back pieces we have cut will fit on without a crack, in order to give a good tone.

The pieces *E*, *D*, and *C* are fastened together with nails or brads, and the front and back pieces are fastened on with brads and glue, if you have it, as in *Figure 4*.

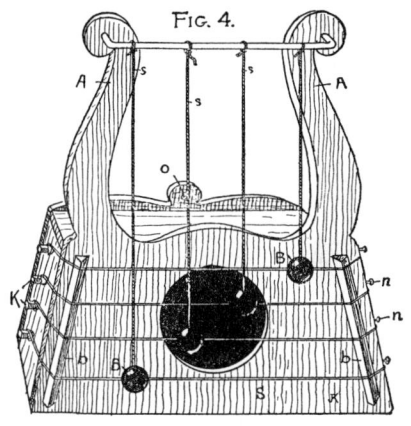

The dotted lines *a* on the pattern show where the bridges go, and these are just three-cornered strips of hard wood with small notches cut at equal distances (say every half inch) for the strings to fit into.

The pegs, *Figure 5*, are of medium hard wood, about a quarter of an inch in diameter at the small end and three-eighths at the large end of the round part *V*, where they flare out into thumb pieces so they can be more easily turned. The holes for them in *E* are bored with the handle end of a file.

Instead of having all the pegs on one end of the box, we arrange three on one end and two on the other so there will be room to turn them. The ends of the strings opposite the pegs are fastened to brads or nails n.

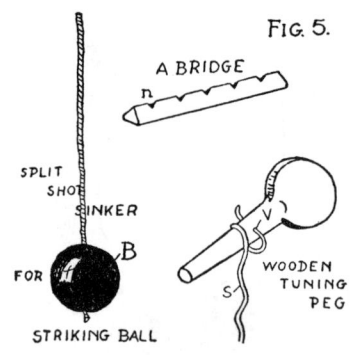

The strings — steel banjo strings — may now be strung up as shown, and tuned to some minor chord that may suit your fancy.

Now get five large lead sinkers — large split shot — and fasten them to five separate pieces of preferably silk thread.

Above, between the arms of the front piece, run a stout wire from the holes b or fasten a wooden rod across; anything that is neat will do, so long as you have something to which you can tie the upper ends of the threads so the balls will hang down and touch the strings.

The threads are now tied on in such a way that there is a lead ball opposite and touching each string below.

A GERMAN "THUR-ZITHER"

Fasten the back of the zither to the hall door by a little strap of tin with a hole in it, that hooks to a nail. Or you can make a little hole in the middle of the top of the sound box at the back to hang it on.

When the door is opened, the strings will be set to swinging and the balls will tap against the wires. The music that results will surprise you.

Before putting on the strings and balls and the steel wires, if you want to give the zither some finish, sandpaper it off carefully and apply shellac varnish. It will need at least four coats, sandpapering the gloss off each coat before adding the next. This will much improve the zither and at the same time help out the tone.

Figure 4 shows a zither with piano pegs at K instead of wooden pegs, and having a back shaped to allow a hole O by which to hang it up.

Figures 2 and *6* show a cigar-box construction which is simpler than this. Here you cut two end pieces E, shaped as shown, and nail them to either end of a cigar box, with a cross piece A at the top. The hole in the cigar box, the bridges, the pegs, and tuning are the same while the balls are supported in the same places

Fig. 6.

by strings fastened from nails along the front edge of the upper piece *A*. This is a much easier thur-zither to make than the first one and will have just as good a tone, but is not quite so handsome in appearance.

A Gutter Water Wheel and Dam

IN the days of melting snows and frequent showers there are plenty of places where a boy can rig up a fine water wheel which can be made of cigar-box wood and which will give considerable power. The drawings show an undershot wheel, but if there is enough height of water from the dam, you can get more power with an overshot wheel, where the water falls on the wheel from above. Ordinarily, however, the undershot is the better.

The dam is simply a big board with a square hole at the center for the water to run through. Other parts of the device include a trough with a frame fastened to it to support a water wheel, and a paddle wheel with buckets or paddles to catch the water.

The trough T is fastened to the dam board D opposite the hole O, so that all the water running through this hole follows the trough. As the water rushes down, it strikes the blades

b of the wheel W and by its force against them turns the wheel.

The board for the dam has the hole near its center so that the lower part can be buried in the ground to prevent the water leaking underneath. The hole, however, is left a little above the ground, so that as great a head of water as possible can pile up against the other side. If water is running in the gutter to a depth of several inches, the dam can be omitted, and the trough merely buried, so that all the gutter water will have to flow through it.

The trough T for a good-sized wheel is made from a cigar box with the top and ends knocked off. The end is nailed to the board dam as in the lower sketch and may be fastened with a block underneath if necessary. The wheel is made of two circles of cigar-box wood with six or eight paddles between.

For this, first cut out the circles, marking them carefully with a compass, then dividing them into, say, six parts, if the wheel is small. Cut six paddles, a couple of inches wide and a little shorter than the width of the trough inside, and nail these around the inside,— the

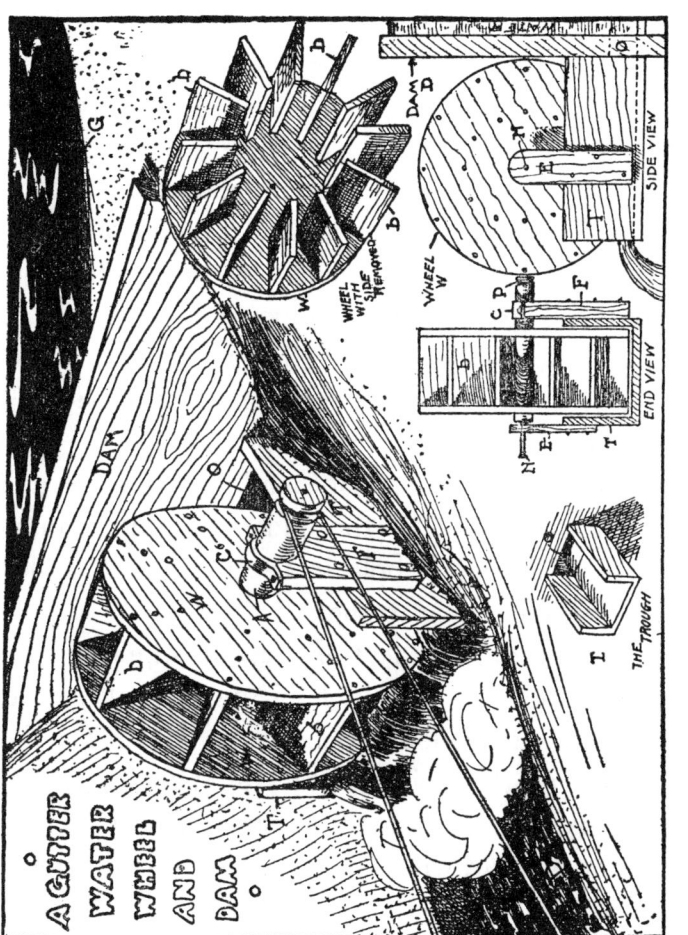

outer edge at the edge of the circle and all pointing in toward the center of the wheel. This can be seen in the upper sketch at the right. The wooden disk or wheel is shown at W and the paddle pieces at b.

When these are nailed in place, the second round piece W is put on, and brads are driven through it into the ends of the paddles b, fastening it. Be sure when you do this to space the paddles evenly, as on the first circle.

The axle is a round stick of wood about half an inch in diameter and an inch longer than the trough is wide. One end pivots on a nail N in the center of the end, this nail running loosely through a hole in the upright E nailed to the side of the trough.

On the other side the shaft is supported by the upright F with a half round part cut at the top into which the axle fits. Over the top a loop of tin C is caught and held on either side by brads or small screws. This is shown in the big drawing as well. This end should fit loosely, for when it gets wet it will swell and stick, if ample room is not left.

If care is taken, the wheel can be made very

GUTTER WATER WHEEL AND DAM

neatly in this fashion, and it should then be painted or dipped in paraffin to prevent warping. The dam, trough, etc., can also be painted to suit the taste. The grooves for the pulley cord can be cut in the axle direct, as shown, or a larger pulley can be fastened on if you want more speed to the belt. This is a toy that any boy can make.

A Water Rocker

I GOT the inspiration for this toy from seeing a patent plate washer in a photographer's shop, and the mechanical movement was so interesting that I went to work and made a toy to work on the same principle.

This toy works by a stream of water, and I have shown it set up with a dam in the gutter so that the water overflowing will rock the toy. This rocking works the rod D back and forth, and you can fasten a saw or any light machinery, like a small pump, to this arm and move it by the power of the rocking.

The principle on which it runs is as follows:

First the box B is made water-tight, with a high partition in its center at P. This box rocks on a bearing n.

Above is the spout or pipe T from which the water runs. As the water comes out of the

A WATER ROCKER

pipe, it runs into the high side of the box and fills it with water, which makes it heavier than the low side, and the high side drops.

THE WATER FLOWS THROUGH THE PIPE T INTO THE HIGH SIDE OF THE BOX B MAKING IT HEAVIER UNTIL IT FALLS AND THE LOW SIDE GOES UP THIS THROWS THE PARTITION P OVER SO THAT THE WATER STILL RUNS INTO THE HIGH SIDE.
THUS THE MILL IS KEPT IN MOTION.

CIGAR BOX ROCKER COMPLETE
FIG. 1

This rocking over of the box brings the partition *P* on the other side of the stream of water, so that now the other side fills until that too is heavier than the low side and the box rocks back. Thus as long as the water runs, the box will rock.

To empty the water on the low side, a valve

-FIG. 2- THE VALVE

V is fixed in each side, like the air valve in the siren whistle described in another chapter, only a nail is driven into the valve V, so when a side drops, the nail hits the board below the box and opens the valve, thus letting the water on the low side run out. When this side rises, the valve closes of its own weight.

The rocker box in the figure is made of a cigar box with a cigar-box wood partition at P. It can be made of two boxes with a tin piece for the partition as in *Figure 3*.

Figure 4 shows the bearing. This is made by nailing a pointed piece of wood, point down, to the side of the box at the center, and pivoting it on the nail shown driven through the hole in the triangular piece into a wooden crosspiece beneath, running under the box between the upright triangular pieces. The

A WATER ROCKER

wooden crosspiece beneath is shown nailed to the board beneath the rocker.

This board is the bottom of a cracker box rigged up for the dam as in *Figure 1*, which

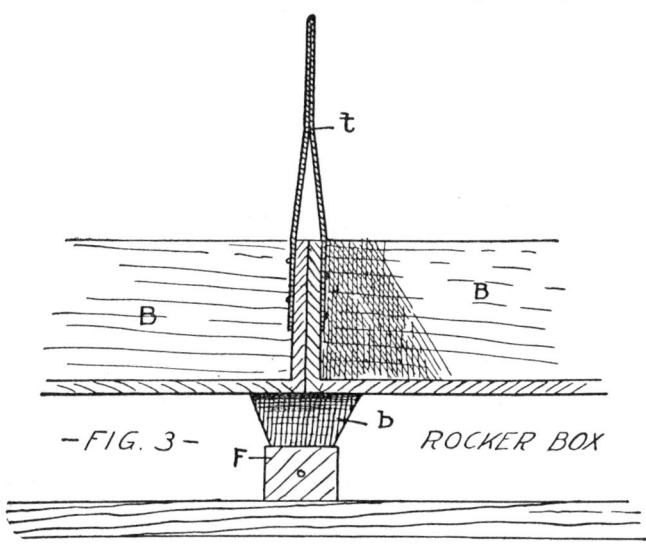

shows the bearing nail at *n* and the triangular piece at *b*.

The pipe *T* runs through a hole in the box at the proper height just above the partition. The box is buried in the dirt to stop the gutter water which must then run through the pipe.

Figure 2 shows how the valve is made of a piece of soft leather *L*, a piece of wood *v* to

217

fasten one edge to the bottom of the rocker box over a hole *O*, and a wooden stiffener *V*.

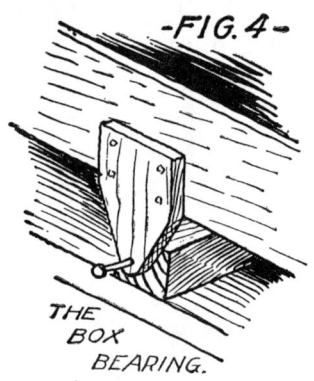
-FIG. 4-
THE BOX BEARING.

A nail *N* through the leather into *V* serves to open the valve when it hits as the box goes down.

This toy can be made to work in the sink by using the water from the tap.

Some Interesting Mechanical Movements

I WISH that every one of my boy readers could enjoy himself for a day in that marvelous place, the South Kensington Museum, where are exhibited all kinds of machines costing hundreds of thousands of dollars, which any visitor may work by merely pushing a button. There are so many things of interest that one would hardly know where to begin to describe them, and there are thousands which of course boys could not attempt to make.

In one of the upper galleries of the museum I once came across a room filled with cases containing all the principal mechanical movements known to engineers. Although you may not care to make these I describe, I have no doubt you will agree that they are interesting for their ingenuity and what they do.

The first one is shown in *Figures 1* and *2*. I will merely explain its working, and you can see from the drawings how to make it, using cigar-box wood for the parts.

When the wheel T is turned by the crank be-

-FIG. 1-

hind, — the bearing for the wheel being in the back board A, — the pins or nails N in its rim catch upon the horizontal part of the bell-crank L. This shoves the square rod R to the right as the wheel turns, as you can see.

When the lever L is moved down half of the distance between two of the nails on T, the nail runs over its end, as in the drawing, *Figure 2*, where the nail is shown just leaving. At the same time the next nail in advance of this one hits a small block b on the right and shoves it back where it started from, or into the position shown by the dotted line.

This nail N then slides off the top of the block b, and just as it does so the lever L has caught up another nail and shoves it back to the right, so that as long as T rotates, the rod

SOME MECHANICAL MOVEMENTS

R will be shoved back and forth, one time for each nail in the wheel *T*.

The guides for the rod and the patterns for the lever *L* are shown in separate drawings, and by making your model as shown and being

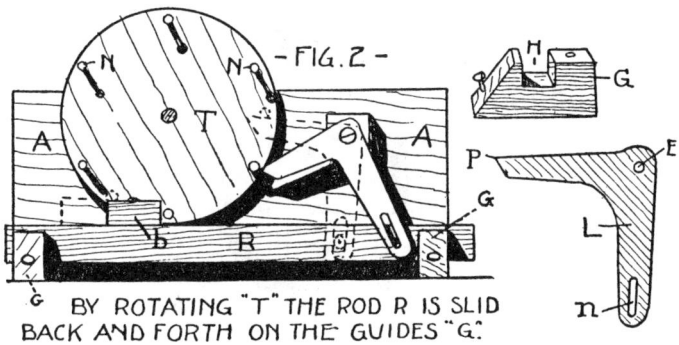

BY ROTATING "T" THE ROD R IS SLID BACK AND FORTH ON THE GUIDES "G"

careful about spacing the nails equal distances apart, you will have no trouble in making a model like this for yourself.

If this is too hard, *Figure 3* shows a simpler way of accomplishing the same thing. In this the rod or frame *A* moves back and forth only three times for one rotation of the wheel *T*.

In this case *T* is a triangular wheel, each side being a curve,— the part of a circle drawn from the point of the opposite side.

This is explained in the smaller drawing,

Figure 3, where *A* is shown as the center of the curve *b–c* which is drawn first. Leave your compasses set as they are, and, taking the point *b* on *b–c*, draw the curve *a–c* with *b* as the

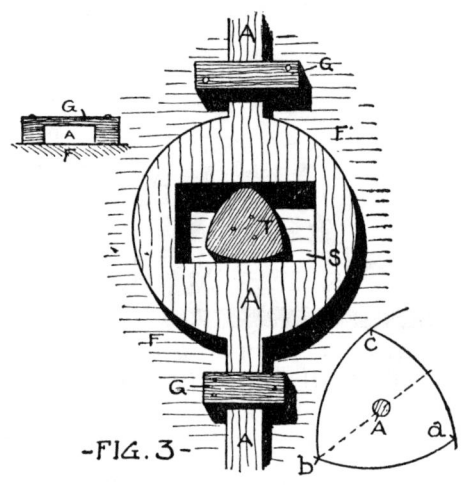

center. Where these two lines cross, you have the point *c*. Taking this as a center and with the same radius, draw *a–b*.

Thus, *b* is the center for *c–a*, *c* is the center for *b–a*, and *a* is the center for *b–c*.

The axle *A* is placed in the center of this wheel, which center is found by running lines across from each corner to the center of the opposite sides, one of these lines being shown

SOME MECHANICAL MOVEMENTS

dotted. Where these three lines cross is the center of the wheel.

Now saw a rectangular hole in a piece of board, as high up and down as the dotted line on the triangle we have just cut, plus one-eighth of an inch, and somewhat wider than it is high. The shape of this hole S is clearly shown in the drawing.

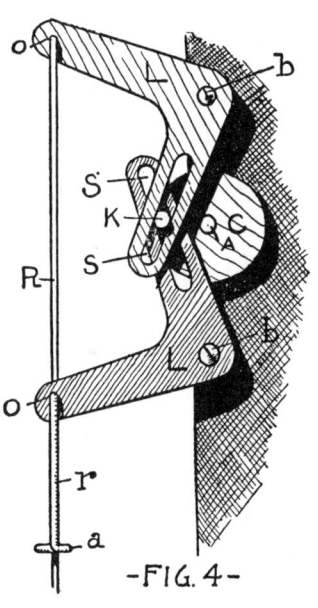

You can saw the outside into a circle as I have shown or leave it in any other shape, but from each side of it run projections, *A*, forming the rod which is to vibrate back and forth. These are held in place by guides *G*, as you can see.

The axle for *T* runs through the back board on which the guides *G* are nailed.

Now, when you turn *T*, each point, as it touches a side will push that side from it.

The point above, in the position shown, has pushed the piece *A* up, but when the wheel turns a little more to the right, one of the points below will begin to push down again, and so it works three times for each turn of *T*.

The third mechanical movement consists, as in *Figure 4*, of a crank *C*, the crank pin being shown at *K* and the axle at *A*.

When *K* revolves in a circle, *K* slides in the slots *S* in one arm of the "bell cranks" *L*, which are on screws at *b*. Thus the crank shoves these levers to the right and left, which in turn works the horizontal ends of the "bell crank" up and down; when the upper one is going up, the lower one is dropping and vice versa.

This principle is used in a double acting pump in which one piston goes up while the other goes down.

Ocean Fun Ashore

NOTE. This toy was invented by the author while watching a crowd playing the game of "Shovelboard" on board the S. S. *Adriatic*.

A STEAMSHIP at sea is not the most quiet place in the world for a person to work in, and this boat is no exception. She's a monster, and the waves affect her as little as any boat afloat, I suppose, and yet, especially in the "Lounge," one can't forget, even while he is absorbed in his work, that just below him is working away at so many revolutions a minute power enough to drive all the street cars of a great city and more besides. If he should forget it for a minute, he will remember it again when his ink bottle starts a war dance on the writing table.

However, I want to tell how you can make a miniature game of "shovelboard" to play at home.

We play it on the ship way up on the boat deck, where the sailors have marked out, about sixty feet apart, two diagrams in chalk like the sketch labeled "marking the board."

Each of the players or sides has four "men," disks of inch wood about five inches in diameter, and a "shovel" stick with which to push them along the deck.

Now, standing at one end of the deck behind the chalked diagram, the first player shoves or slides his first man at the farther diagram across the deck, trying to make it stop on the largest figure on the diagram, which is, as you see, "10 on." If he goes too far into that last section, it is "10 off" and that much is taken from his score.

Any "man" stopping on a line of any kind does not count; to count, they must be well within the end circles or squares. These squares measured about ten inches each way.

The player who scored a hundred first was the winner, and it was great sport.

Maybe you can mark this board on the asphalt somewhere and play the game, but it is hard to find a place large and smooth enough. Here's a way to make one on a small scale, only you must make a toy man to shove the shovel for you.

OCEAN FUN ASHORE

Here he is in *Figure 1*, mounted on a small base *C*. The body part *A* is fast to *C* by the

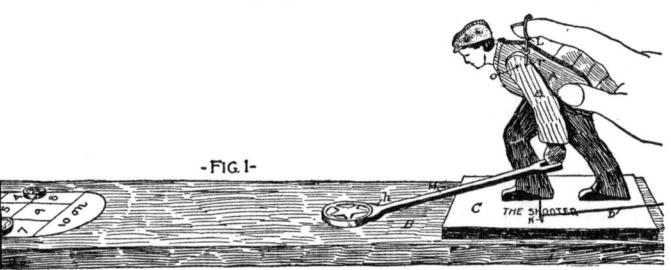

feet, and the arm *a* is pivoted on a small nail to turn at the shoulders at *O*.

Fastened to the arm just back of *O* at *r* is a wire *L* which ends in a loop into which the index finger is to fit, the thumb and middle finger grasping the body. Then by working the index finger

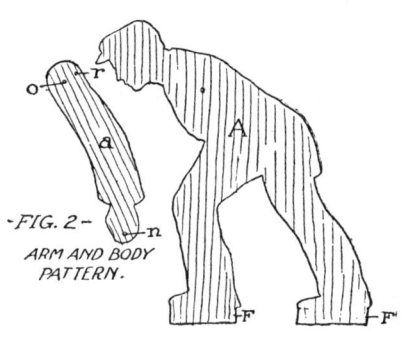

up and down, the arm *a* will swing forward and back.

To the hand below at *n*, *Figure 2*, the "shovel" is fastened, and by shoving down on

L as shown, the shovel H will be thrust sharply forward and slide the checker men — used in place of the disks for the large game — across our toy board.

For a "board" use a flat board of any kind,

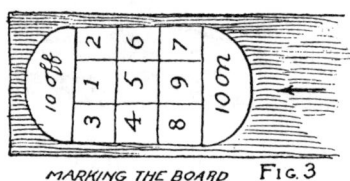
MARKING THE BOARD   FIG. 3

and the diagram need be marked off only at one end. The squares should be about twice as big as your checker men, and the length of the board will depend on how far your toy shooter-man can shove. You can tell by trying him a few times.

The shooter-man himself is cut out of thin wood by a pattern enlarged from the one shown. The lugs F on the man's feet fit into holes in the base C and are fastened there. The base C is left free to be set in any

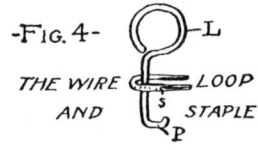
-FIG. 4-
THE WIRE AND LOOP STAPLE

position on the board where the player may wish to put it.

The "shovel" H is just a straight, thin stick formed in a sort of head to fit the curve of the

OCEAN FUN ASHORE

men it shoves. The other end is cut "crotched" to pivot to the hand by a pin at *n*. Be sure that all the joints work easily, but are not too loose.

Fig. 5 — THE SHOVEL   H'

If you want to use a different method of working the arm and one which is perhaps a little simpler, drive a small nail into the arm at *r* instead of using the wire *L*. Then from this run a string down through a staple *K* in the base below and back.

Then by holding *C* down with the left hand and jerking the string *D* with the right, the hand will be shoved forward with more power.

If you use *L*, a staple should be driven into *A* as shown in *Figure 4*, to keep it loosely in place.

Fighting Wild Irishmen

I WAS over in Ireland once on an Orange Day, and the people were certainly having a great time. On this particular day another young fellow and myself were on our bicycles in the northern part of the island, and every village we came to had its own peculiar demonstration. There were orange bands in evidence everywhere, worn in profusion, and drunks aplenty! And such fights! Maybe that is where I got the idea for this fighting toy.

Here are the fighters, full size, and you can trace the illustrations, that is, the body part, paste them on cigar-box wood, and cut down the wood.

The arms can be traced separately, for they are cut of separate pieces and pivoted at the shoulders to turn.

The front foot of each man has a round part below, about an inch and a half across. You can see this in *Figure 1*, which shows the

fighters complete and ready to start; but *Figure 2* shows the details.

When you get the men cut out, you had better make the base stick B. This is about an inch wide, half an inch thick, and eighteen inches long. Notches O, a quarter of an inch wide and about two inches long, are cut in this stick toward the center and far enough apart for the fighters to reach each other easily — say two and a half inches apart.

Now stick the front foot of the man in one of these slots and pivot it with a brad n so that it turns easily. Where the circle part sticks out below the stick, cut a notch N, *Figure 3*, below and at the back, so that a rubber band stretched between the two notches will hold the men up, with the back foot f resting on the stick to keep the men from leaning too far back. You can see how the foot f rests on the stick in *Figure 3* while the front foot F sticks down through the notch.

The rubber band is shown at R.

At H, on the other side of the circular part underneath, make a hole and run a string through as at S, having it long enough so that you can work the toy as in *Figure 2*, with the thumbs in the loops of the string. The thumbs will pull the string and stretch the band *R* as the men go toward each other.

The arms are fastened on with little wire loops at each end so the arm pieces can't slip off. Then, when you pull the strings and the body of the man moves, the arms will flap and swing around in the most dangerous-looking manner.

A Fighting Rooster Toy

AFTER you have made the Fighting Wild Irishman out of cigar-box wood you will understand very easily how to make the "Rooster Fight" toy shown in the accompanying drawing. The principle of operation is almost exactly the same, the chief difference being the shape of the figures supposed to be fighting.

The base stick, shown at D in this case, has a little round pan like the cover to a blacking box fastened to its center at P. This is supposed to contain the food over which the roosters are fighting. The base stick has slots cut at S and at O so that the roosters' feet and the trigger pieces T can fit into place.

The drawing shows the shape of the pieces which make up each rooster; but notice that the rooster legs L pivot on a nail d between the wing pieces W and the body pieces B.

Just forward of the wings a little connecting wire C is run between a hole h in the main

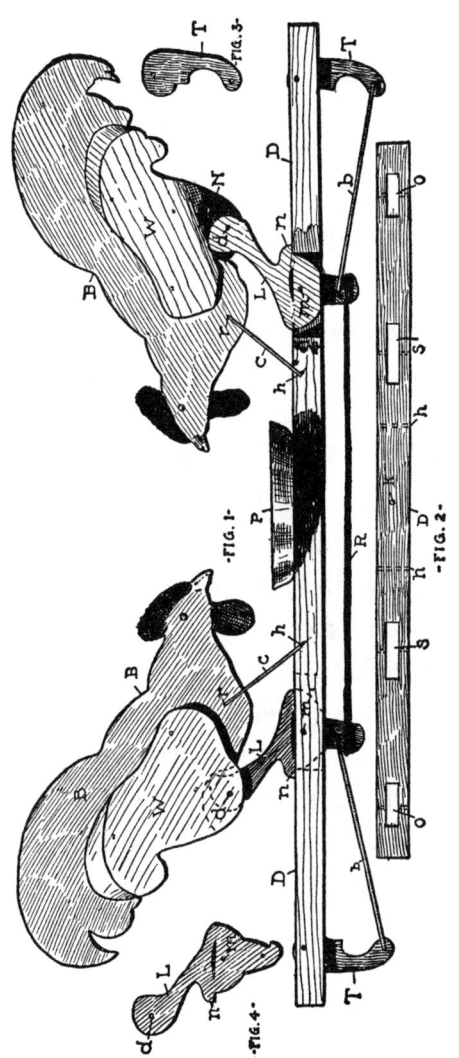

stick and a hole *r* in the rooster's body. These holes are so arranged that the distance between *d* and *r* is the same between *m* and *h*.

Notice also the hook *n* cut in the back part of the rooster's foot to keep it from pulling back too far through the action of the rubber band *R*.

The drawing shows very plainly also the patterns for the trigger or thumb pieces *T* at either end.

The pieces *b* are wires running between the lower part of the foot pattern to the thumb pieces *T* by which the toy is operated. The whole mechanism is worked exactly like the Fighting Irishman toy, as shown in *Figure 2* of the previous story.

It is hardly necessary to explain that the figures are cut out of cigar-box wood, although the main base stick is half an inch thick and an inch wide.

A Climbing Bear

NO toy for a long while has enjoyed such continued popularity as the Teddy Bear. A toy of this kind which will climb a string all by itself merely by alternately pulling and releasing the string, as shown in *Figure 1*, can easily be made.

Figure 2 shows the Teddy Bear with one of the cigar-box sides so that the mechanism can be seen, also the bear completed and some of the separate parts.

The arms *P* are fastened securely by nails *m* to the body part of the bear. The two arms stick out in front and have between the paws a loop of chamois skin *C*, as shown in the small drawing, with a string running through the loop. A small nail driven through the paws and through this chamois skin holds the string tightly between the arm pieces. The leg pieces *L* are pivoted on a nail at *N* and have between them, — outside of the body, —

BOY'S BOOK OF MECHANICAL MODELS

-FIG. 1-

two little round wooden pieces r. These disks have grooves around their rim and act like pulleys which do not turn.

A CLIMBING BEAR

The string which runs through the chamois skin runs under the piece r nearer the body and over the second one out in the heel. Details of this construction are shown in small sketches.

On one side of the bear are fastened two nails T with a rubber band between. One is in the arms above, and one — a small tack — in the position shown in the leg piece below, so that when the lower leg piece L is up in the position shown in the lower drawing, *Figure 2*, the two nails T and the pivoting nail N are in line.

Now when you pull tight on the string, as shown in *Figure 1*, the chamois C and the lower outer roller r are in line. The pull on the cord tends to pull the two rollers r into line with C, but the string cramps on the rollers and will not slide, so that, as you pull, the chamois allows the string to slip through it, and the paws move up the string. This stretches the rubber R which has been fixed between the two nails T.

When you release the tension on the string, it becomes slack and has no friction on the rollers r, although the chamois C is still tight enough to hold the weight of the toy. The rubber band is now free to pull the legs up to the horizontal position again, allowing the string to slip past the rollers, and the lower legs to climb up a step. Thus, by alternately pulling and releasing the string, first the paws and then the legs slide up the string, and the bear quickly climbs to the top. This toy is very lifelike in its movements and very funny.

In making the bear, enlarge the patterns and shape shown in these drawings, on cigar-box wood, and cut them out with a jackknife or fret saw.

When fixing the chamois skin in place, get the nail in just tight enough to hold the weight of the toy without slipping. A slight tap on the paws with a hammer will tighten the hold at any time, and you can loosen the adjustment by prying apart with a chisel or knife.

Have the rollers r tight between the lower leg pieces; these you cut of cigar-box wood, making the central hole first. The nails go through this hole, and these hold the legs far enough apart so that they do not bind on the body part.

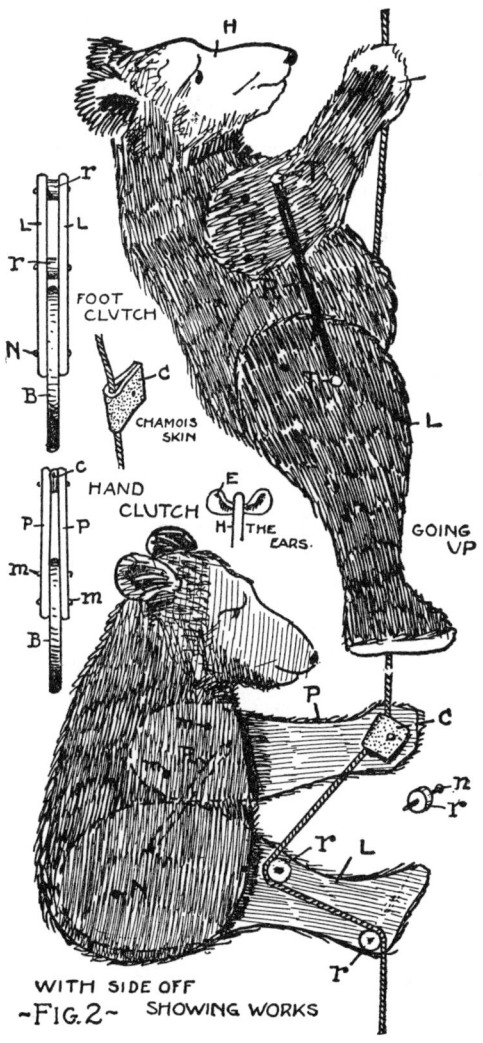

FIG. 2 — WITH SIDE OFF SHOWING WORKS

When the toy is done, cover it with fuzzy cloth as shown, — Canton flannel will do, — and you will have a very lifelike bear. This was first made by a boy friend of mine and worked perfectly. I have seen dozens of them since made by other boys, and they were all great successes.

A Wiggle Bug

THIS toy, when drawn across the floor, wiggles and twists in a lifelike and terrifying manner, and all by the action of a common spool peculiarly fixed.

The body of the bug has fastened to it at the front by pivots a head part, as at H, to which are attached the front legs L and a tail part T with the hind legs fastened thereto. In the body part between the two is a spool S with a slanting groove N in it, and the weight rests on this spool when the toy is in motion.

This spool is pivoted on nail bearings n in side pieces t, shown dotted in *Figure 1*, so that when the toy is drawn over the floor, the spool revolves. Fastened to the head piece, as at m, — driven into the rear end of it, in fact, — is a nail whose head rests in the slanting groove N in the spool S. The head part pivots at b, turning on a nail at this point, so that now you can understand the action.

BOY'S BOOK OF MECHANICAL MODELS

When the spool S turns, the nail head must follow it from side to side. As the nail *m* is moved from side to side on its head end by the groove, the head of the toy, on the other

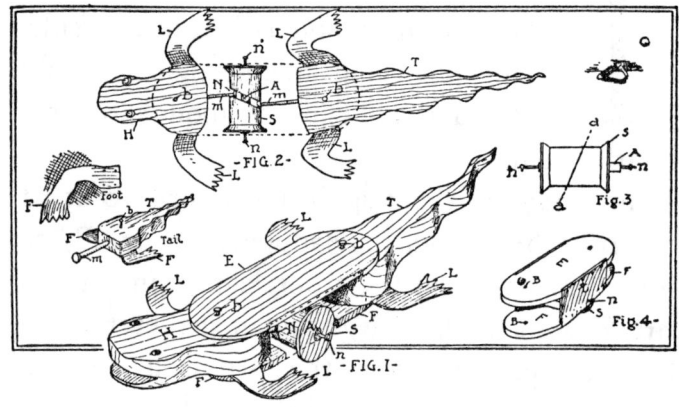

end, is wiggled from side to side on the pivot *b*, with the legs attached to it moving at the same time in a very lifelike manner.

In the same way the tail part is fixed, pivoted at a point *b* also, and with a nail *m* bearing in the same groove *N* of the spool. The tail part will move in the opposite direction from the head, however, as the nail working it will be on the opposite side of the groove. It is this opposite motion which gives the toy

A WIGGLE BUG

its lifelike appearance as you draw it across the floor.

The body part of the bug is made of cigar-box wood, the top and bottom piece being made semicircular at each end with a hole for the pivot nail at *B*. The lower piece *F* has an opening for the spool to stick through.

The head and tail pieces are cut of inch wood, and weight will not hinder, for the toy will need enough weight so that the spool will turn and not slide when it is drawn across the floor. Make the legs *L* of tin or pasteboard and fasten them in place with small tacks.

The spool part is easily fixed. First get a large spool. Saw across it an at angle as by the line *a–d* in *Figure 3*. Then fit a tight wooden axle to the spool, spreading the halves of the spool apart so that a space a little wider than the head of the nail you are going to use for *m* is left between. Then set the spool to the shaft with glue. Nails *n* in the centers of the shaft ends will act as pivots for the spool.

The rest of the making can be easily understood from the drawing. When the nails *m* are set, be sure they are in the slot in the spool at just the right depth, and that they do not bind while turning in the spools.

The amount of fun one can have with this toy depends on its lifelike appearance, so be careful in making it.

A Wooden Elephant

BOB EVANS was up against quite a proposition. He had only ten cents and the next day was his little brother's birthday. He wanted to give his little brother a present, but he didn't feel that ten cents would get very much, so his first move was to look up the author in his workshop and tell him his troubles.

"I think," said I, "that we can fix up something which will be great fun, and you can save your ten cents as well. I used to make a whole lot of cut-out toys from wood for some of the younger children, and there is no reason why you can't make some of these yourself.

"Wait till I get my scrapbook, and I think you will find something there that will please the youngster."

From the shelf in the corner of my shop, I took down one of my scrapbooks and, thumbing over the pages, came finally to the set of drawings shown in this chapter.

"Now here is an elephant that wabbles his head and trunk when you wheel him along the floor, and it is a very lifelike toy at that.

FIG. 1.

It can be made any size for which you have wood."

Bob was interested at once, and looked the drawings over very carefully.

"I think I can see right away," said he, "just how this works; but I don't think I could draw the elephant good enough."

"That's easy," I told him, "for I can show you how to copy this drawing. You see from

A WOODEN ELEPHANT

Figure 1 just how this toy is made and just what kind of work you will have to do in making it.

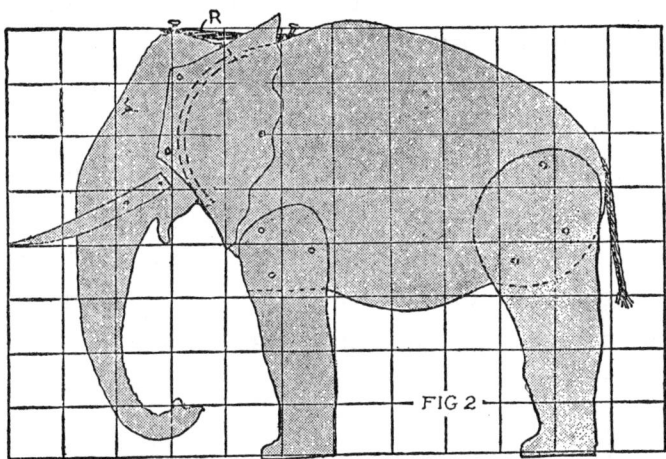

"In the first place it runs on wheels on a base, a great deal like the toys you buy at the stores, only this is simpler to make. The main body parts are cut out of inch wood, while the legs and ears are cut out of thin cracker-box wood and nailed on.

"*Figure 2* gives you a pattern of all the parts, which can be traced off separately after the elephant has been drawn to scale. Any one can copy this pattern, even if he is a very poor artist, for all you have to do is to make up a set of 1-inch squares like *Figure 2* and copy one square at a time, being sure that each line is in the proper square and runs to the proper point in that square.

"For instance, the eye is in third square to the right and the second square down, and is a little to the left of the center of that square. The lower part of the trunk is on the upper edge of the fourth bottom square to the right. Starting at this point, you can follow along, one square at a time, entering and leaving each square at the proper place until the whole elephant is complete.

"Then it is very easy to trace off each part separately, as shown,—the body, the trunk, the legs, the ears, and the tusks.

"There is but one pattern each for the body and trunk. Two ears are made, however, and two each of the front and hind legs. Also two tusks are made of very thin wood. Pieces for the front and hind legs can be cut out of inch stuff, and then sawed down the middle and planed off, which will make both of these patterns exactly the same.

A WOODEN ELEPHANT

"These parts should be carefully smoothed off and sandpapered before they are put together, but they will look better if the corners are left square instead of being rounded off.

"The ears fasten to the trunk and the trunk part is pivoted to the body through the ears, as shown by the dotted lines in *Figure 2*.

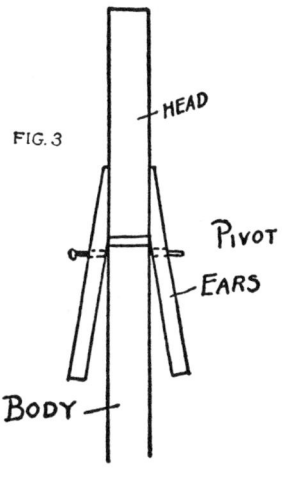

"The body part slips between these ears, and a nail through holes in the proper places shown in *Figure 3*, pivots the trunk at this point. The trunk does not balance to this center, but will hang off to one side until a rubber band R, in *Figure 2*, is fitted between nails on the head and trunk to hold this in proper position and act as a string for its action.

"This is a little ahead of my description, however, for we have not yet put together the trunk and head of the animal. These are nailed in place as shown, and if glue is also added, the toy will be so much stronger.

After the elephant is put together entirely, a strip of wood S is slipped between the feet lengthwise, and nailed in place, and this strip is nailed to a baseboard B made of inch stuff fitted with wheels as shown, which forms the standard for the toy. By this means the elephant can be drawn around by a string, his head bobbing this way and that through the jerking of the motion, making a very lifelike imitation of Barnum and Bailey's big creature.

"That's great," said Bob, "for now I can fix up my little brother, have some fun myself making this toy, and still have my ten cents left."

"That may be," I told him, "but don't forget to give the toy a coat of gray house-paint when it is done, and take care that the paint does not get into the joints too much. After this is dry you can put in the eye with black paint and add the few wrinkles which an elephant needs to look natural.

"Also you can tack a piece of rope on for a

A WOODEN ELEPHANT

tail, and screw a screw eye into the front end of the base block for the string which will draw the toy across the floor.

"When this is done, your brother will have a toy as good as any he can buy."

A Submarine Boat

ANY boy can make a submarine boat of small size which will go down to the bottom of the lake or river and then come up again of itself, as shown in *Figure 1*.

The body of this toy is sawed out of inch wood into the shape of a submarine about two feet long.

In outline it is sausage shape with a little special hump on top shaped like a boat, which is meant to stick out of the water when the toy is floating. On top of this a round stick gives the appearance of a periscope.

At the rear are some rudders made of tin, while in the center is a sort of triangular box pivoted on some bearings at the bottom and held upright in place by a little trigger.

The stones in the box form a weight, and enough are put in so that they will just sink the boat when it is set in the water. After the stones are in, set the trigger to hold the box from upsetting. When the submarine is fixed

A SUBMARINE BOAT

this way and put in the water, it sinks, and as it sinks, the rudders steer it forward. The minute it gets to the bottom, or near the bottom, the lower arm of this trigger or lever, *T*,

COMPLETED SUBMARINE ABOUT TO STRIKE BOTTOM

in *Figure 1*, strikes bottom, and thus pulls itself out of the notch in the top of the weight box *P*. When this trigger is released, the box is pivoted on its lower corner, and immediately the weight in the box upsets it and dumps all the stones out, as shown in *Figure 2*.

Now, when these stones are out, the submarine is light enough to float, and it comes

BOY'S BOOK OF MECHANICAL MODELS

to the surface, the weight of the tin box and trigger below keeping it right side up.

Figures 2, 3, and *4* show details of the boat and how it is put together.

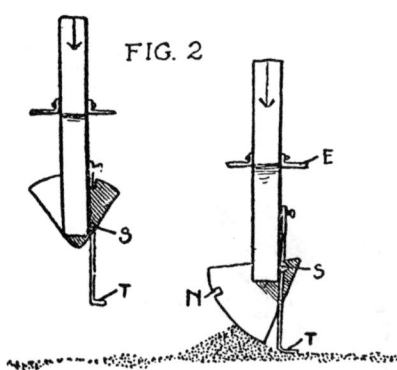

FIG. 2

The patterns can be enlarged to proper size, folded on the dotted lines, and put together for the various parts.

On the toy here I have used a short metal lever, *T*, and trigger, as you can see, with a guide to hold it close to the frame of the submarine, but in

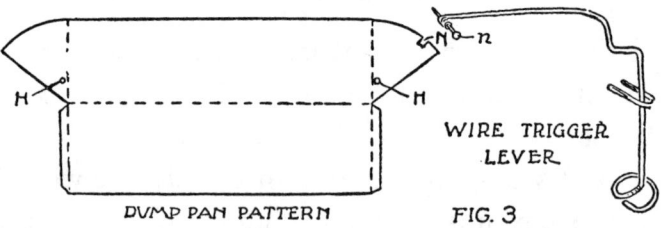

DUMP PAN PATTERN FIG. 3 WIRE TRIGGER LEVER

Figure 3 I show how this trigger can be made of wire with a staple to hold it in place and a handle on one end for a pivot. By its own

A SUBMARINE BOAT

weight the flat part of this wire will drop into the notch *N*, of the dump pan, and hold it from upsetting. This dump pan pivots on a wire running through the holes *H*, and out through little tin-bearing pivots *S*, shown in the drawings in *Figure 4*.

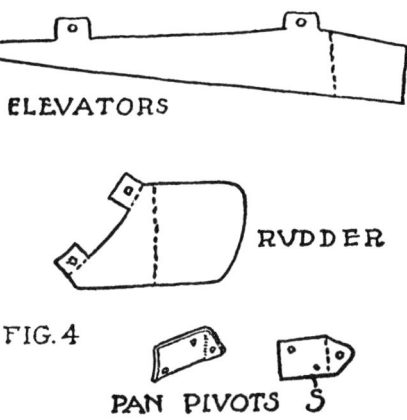

These are made of tin cut to shape with an old pair of scissors.

A study of the drawings will tell you more than words, but if you want some fun, make some of these submarines and see which can dive the deepest and still come to the surface again.

And, by the way, by timing this toy with a stopwatch to a ten-foot depth and using this as a standard of comparison, then you can tell how deep any part of the lake is by noting the time it takes your submarine to go down to the bottom and come up again.